DURHAM EXECUTIONS
FROM 1700 TO 1900

By the same author

Foul Deeds and Suspicious Deaths in and Around Newcastle
Foul Deeds and Suspicious Deaths in and Around Durham
Foul Deeds and Suspicious Deaths Around the Tees
Executions and Hangings in Newcastle and Morpeth
Bygone Seaton Carew
Shipwrecks from the Tees to the Tyne
Durham Executions: The Twentieth Century (forthcoming)

DURHAM EXECUTIONS

FROM 1700 to 1900

MAUREEN ANDERSON

Wharncliffe Books

First Published in Great Britain in 2007 by
Wharncliffe Books
an imprint of
Pen and Sword Books Ltd
47 Church Street
Barnsley
South Yorkshire
S70 2AS

© Maureen Anderson 2007

ISBN: 978-1-84563-025-6

Typeset in 10/12pt Plantin by Concept, Huddersfield.

Printed and bound in England by
Biddles Ltd.

Pen and Sword Books Ltd incorporates the Imprints of
Pen & Sword Aviation, Pen & Sword Maritime,
Pen & Sword Military, Wharncliffe Books,
Pen & Sword Select, Pen and Sword Military Classics
and Leo Cooper.

For a complete list of Pen & Sword titles please contact
PEN & SWORD BOOKS LIMITED
47 Church Street
Barnsley
South Yorkshire
S70 2AR
England
E-mail: enquiries@pen-and-sword.co.uk
Website: www.pen-and-sword.co.uk

Contents

Individual Pet Cremation Service

pdsa — SINCE 1917
SAVING PETS CHANGING LIVES

Our service

Your pet will be cremated on its own by CPC with the utmost dignity.

After the individual cremation, the ashes of your pet will be carefully placed into a beech casket or scattering tube, and returned to you by Courier Service. You will also receive a signed sympathy card, which confirms details of your pet's individual cremation.

What do I need to do?

Your pet will be collected from the PDSA for individual cremation and will be taken to (vet to tick):

☐ Cambridge Pet Crematorium – 01763 207700

☑ Caledonian Pet Crematorium – 01506 833686

☐ Cheltenham Pet Crematorium – 01684 857494

Please telephone the crematorium, ticked above, to speak to one of CPC's bereavement advisors to confirm arrangements for your pet's cremation and to arrange payment.

If you would like to attend your pet's cremation to say goodbye it is important that you contact the crematorium prior to the collection of your pet from the PDSA.

Option 1

Emerald Scattering Tube

This attractive bio-degradable scattering tube is ideal and simple to use for the scattering of ashes.

Small pet	£58.00 +P&P
Cat	£68.00 +P&P
Small dog	£76.00 +P&P
Medium dog	£86.00 +P&P
Large dog	£98.00 +P&P
Extra large dog	£109.00 +P&P

Option 2

Beech Casket

A elegant hand crafted beech casket, with a brass nameplate, for the safe keeping of ashes.

Small pet	£70.00 +P&P
Cat	£80.00 +P&P
Small dog	£88.00 +P&P
Medium dog	£98.00 +P&P
Large dog	£110.00 +P&P
Extra large dog	£121.00 +P&P

Postage		
	Small pets, cats, small and medium dogs	£10.74
	Large and extra large dogs	£16.15

Prices inclusive of VAT. Ashes are returned back by Courier Service and will require a signature upon delivery. Prices correct at time of print. Other caskets are for sale at cpccares.com.

pdsa.org.uk

About CPC

At CPC, we care

Each pet that comes into our lives and fills our hearts with warmth deserves to be remembered.

We understand the special bond between you and your pet, which is why we extend our hand to you with kindness and compassion.

As one of the oldest family-run pet crematoria, CPC cares and respects your individual needs as a bereaved pet owner. Performing our first individual cremation in 1981, you can be assured that all aspects of our service are carried out with dignity and to the highest standard.

Here to help

We are here to answer any questions or concerns you may have about your pet's individual cremation and the return of your pet's ashes. Please contact the crematorium ticked overleaf for information and advice.

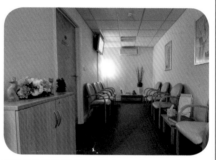

CPC Crematoria

Cambridge Pet Crematorium

A505 Main Road, Thriplow Heath, Nr Royston
Hertfordshire SG8 7RR
T: 01763 207700   E: cambridge@cpccares.com

Caledonian Pet Crematorium

Unit 15, Nettlehill Road, Houstoun Industrial Estate,
Livingston, West Lothian EH54 5DL
T: 01506 833686   E: caledonian@cpccares.com

Cheltenham Pet Crematorium

Unit 5601, Shannon Place, Shannon Way, Tewkesbury
Gloucestershire GL20 8SL
T: 01684 857494   E: cheltenham@cpccares.com

Ref. CPC-ALL-161017

cpccares.com

Introduction

An uneasy hush settles over the room; the jury brings in a verdict of guilty; the judge dons a black cap and, after summing up the case that has been heard before him, the dreaded words of doom echo around the court:

> *The sentence of the court upon you is that you be taken from this place to a lawful prison and thence to a place of execution and that you be hanged by the neck until you are dead; and that your body be afterwards buried within the precincts of the prison in which you shall be confined before your execution. And may the Lord have mercy on your soul. Amen. Take him (or her) down.*

In the eighteenth and nineteenth centuries men from all over England, Scotland, Ireland and even other parts of the world flocked to County Durham, bringing their families with them, to work in the many coal and iron mines that were being opened. In 1845, a disease had blighted the potato crops in Ireland. This meant that many families were starving so the opportunity of a wage, however meagre, was not only necessary to sustain life but was also an extremely attractive option. Families were accommodated in cramped, inadequate and unsanitary housing. Beer houses and inns were numerous and the wages that were earned were often spent on alcohol rather than improving the quality of life. Domestic violence and drunken brawls were rife and sometimes resulted in death. With little form of education on birth control families were large and, although many children died at birth or in infancy, those that survived had to be fed. Children were neglected and often went hungry because their mothers were drinking alongside their fathers. The life that was led by many was born of a deep despair of their daily drudge, surroundings and continuous poverty.

In the poorer working classes women were held in very low esteem and it is probable that some domestic killings went undetected through lack of interest from those living around them and from the relevant officials. Throughout the nineteenth century many of the felons that were executed at Durham were responsible for the murder of a wife or sweetheart. If a woman was killed, especially if she was of 'dissolute habits', it was thought by many to be that she caused her own demise by provocation of one sort or another and there were often recommendations of mercy for the perpetrator by the jury. The twentieth century was dawning before women began to have more rights but violence within households was still almost ignored by the law – except in extreme cases. It is only comparatively recently that 'zero tolerance' on domestic violence has been put into place. Mercy was also often recommended in cases where the man was drunk as it was believed alcohol caused a person to act out of character, so they were considered temporarily insane or of a diseased mind and therefore not wholly responsible for their actions. Reprieves, however, were rarely granted.

Prior to the nineteenth century about 220 crimes were considered capital offences. These included burglary, sacrilege, writing threatening letters, being in the company of gypsies for one month, adopting a disguise, stealing a handkerchief or shooting a rabbit. There were about twenty-five offences which could all see the perpetrator facing the end of a rope. There was no form of appeal and the executions were carried out within days, on some occasions just hours, of the death sentence being passed. The early nineteenth century saw changes to these harsh laws and gradually it was only for the more serious crimes that the death penalty was invoked. Hanging for shoplifting was abolished in 1818 and for housebreaking and theft of livestock between 1819 and 1833. The Punishment of Death Act (1832) reduced the number of capital crimes by about two-thirds and gibbeting was abolished in 1843. The Criminal Law Consolidation Act (1861) resulted in further changes. The death penalty was then limited to the crimes of murder, treason, arson and piracy with violence. Murder was the only crime in peacetime to be punishable by death. In these cases the law dictated that the courts had to impose the extreme penalty and could only give a recommendation for mercy. It was then up to the prisoner and his defence to appeal to the Home Secretary – and the later established Criminal Court of Appeal.

In 1868 a law was passed against the practice of public executions. The gallows had to be erected within the prison walls and the execution witnessed only by the officials concerned. On some occasions the press were still allowed to be present and a detailed (and often exaggerated) report would be published in the newspapers of the time. Allowing access to members of the press was up to the justices and on a few occasions in the nineteenth and twentieth centuries this was denied. The last execution held at Durham where the press were permitted to attend was in 1910.

Once the sentence had been completed the body was left to hang for an hour and, when cut down, would be placed in an open coffin after which an inquest was held. Besides a sworn jury at the inquest there would only be a doctor and officials present. Abolitionists of the death penalty believed that the inquests were a farce as the public could be kept in ignorance as to whether the condemned person died instantaneously or in agony.

Social divisions were great in the eighteenth and nineteenth centuries and yet, when it came to a murder trial, all protocol seemed to disappear. There are many reports of the gallery of the Assizes being packed with 'ladies of quality' jostling for seating space amongst the rabble. Likewise, at the public executions, fine hats, parasols and gloves would be seen side by side with filthy aprons and heavy footwear.

Until the twentieth century there was no knowledge of blood grouping and little in the way of forensics. The meat for the table was often killed by the man of the house and, as hygiene was not a priority, bloodstains would sometimes remain on the clothing for days. If a stain that resembled blood was found it could not be ascertained whether it was animal or human or, sometimes, if it was indeed blood at all. In many cases the accused was found guilty on sparse circumstantial evidence and there is no doubt that a few of the individuals that went to the gallows were innocent.

Many of those that were hanged were victims of their circumstances and their environments. While this can not be used as an excuse for taking another human life, the cases related here will, hopefully, give the reader an insight into the harsh and uncompromising lives that led to the terrible crimes perpetrated by some of our ancestors.

Grateful acknowledgement and thanks are due to the following for their assistance during the compilation of this book: the pleasant and ever helpful staff of Hartlepool Reference Library; staff of Durham Clayport Library; all at Wharncliffe Books; Brian Elliott, Series Editor, for his invaluable comments and directions; Peter and Margaret Fox for their assistance with background history and my husband, Jim, for his enduring patience and support.

CHAPTER 1

Executioners

Although numerous broadsheets concerning the crime and sentence were printed and sold at early executions they rarely contained the name of the executioner. The records that have survived giving the names of the men who carried out the sentence of the law seldom link them with a particular execution. It is known, however, that many of the early executioners were often convicted felons themselves who would be given the option of a pardon or a lighter sentence to carry out the deed. One example is William Gardner who had been sentenced to death for sheep stealing. Gardner received the offer of transportation instead of the noose for carrying out the unsavoury task of hanging William Winter, Jane and Eleanor Clark at Newcastle in 1792. They had been sentenced for the robbery and murder of Margaret Crozier. Records became more complete in the mid-nineteenth century as newspaper reports made almost as much of the arrival and departure of the executioner as the execution itself. A few of the literate executioners wrote their memoirs which were published in book form and survive to give a clear insight into both their personal involvement and the impersonal side of their work.

William Calcraft was born in 1800 in the village of Baddow near Chelmsford. Being the eldest of twelve children he would have sought employment at an early age. After trying several

William Calcraft, 1800–79, held the office of executioner from 1829–74, the longest serving of any British hangman. He is recorded to have performed at least six executions, including one double, at Durham. Here Calcraft poses for his photo at the age of seventy.
Author's collection

different jobs, none of which were to his liking, he began to hawk food to the crowds at the frequent executions that took place in London. In 1828, now married and even more in need of permanent employment, he successfully applied to become an executioner. Calcraft went down in the annals of executioners with two claims to fame. The first was his 'short drop' which caused most of his victims to die painfully by strangulation, or where the rope would break and the terrified victim would have to stand on the trap yet again. His second claim to fame was that he was the longest serving executioner, in office for almost forty-five years, between 1829–74. Calcraft was pensioned off against his will and became a virtual recluse after complaining loudly to the media – or anyone else that would listen – concerning the unfair treatment he had received from the authorities. He died at his home in December 1879.

Thomas Askern was from York and had been imprisoned in York Castle for debt. He was about forty when he took up the post of hangman in 1856 because Calcraft was busy elsewhere and a replacement was needed immediately for an impending execution. Like Calcraft, Askern was not particularly competent at his work as there were many reports of a felon struggling at the end of the rope before death. He remained in office until 1877 and died in December 1878. Askern often worked in the north of England, as did George Smith who was born in Dudley in 1805 and was in office from 1849–73. Smith performed his last execution in August 1872. He had been a prisoner in Stafford gaol when he entered the trade as assistant to Calcraft. Smith was renowned for wearing a long white coat and tall hat when performing his official duty.

William Marwood was born at Horncastle in Lincolnshire in 1820. Although a cobbler by trade he took an interest in the methods of

execution used by the hangmen and, assisting Calcraft, felt that he could perform a hanging far more humanely. Marwood is credited with inventing the 'long drop'. This meant that if a person's weight was calculated against the length of rope used the neck would be broken,

William Marwood, 1820–83, held the office of executioner from 1874–83 and performed seven executions, including one triple, at Durham. Courtesy of Brian Elliott

so death would be quicker for the prisoner and less stressful for those watching. In fact, strangulation was still the cause of death using the long drop, but the broken neck would render the person unconscious for those final minutes. Marwood was fifty-four when he carried out his first hanging and everything went so smoothly that he was appointed official hangman. He performed 176 executions throughout his nine years of service. He died in 1883 of inflammation of the lungs.

Bartholomew Binns acted as Marwood's assistant at double executions and took over as Chief Executioner in 1883. Formal complaints about his drunkenness and incompetence had him removed from office after only a year although he did later act as assistant at several executions.

James Berry was born at Heckmondwike in Yorkshire in 1852. He was working as a policeman in Bradford when he met William Marwood. Like Marwood, Berry had also worked out tables based on the weight of the prisoner and these calculations became more refined. Throughout his official term, from 1884–92, he carried out approximately 200 hangings. For all his attention to detail not

all of his executions went smoothly. At least three prisoners strangled to death, two men were very nearly decapitated and one actually was. The authorities were always pleased when an admission of guilt was procured from the condemned man. Until a policy of secrecy surrounding executions came into force the confession would be published in the newspapers to prove that justice had been served. Even after the secrecy policy a confession of guilt would sometimes mysteriously leak out. Berry, a nonconformist preacher, was encouraged to press the condemned men into admitting guilt and repenting their sin. He was the

James Berry, 1852–1913, held the office of executioner from 1884–92. On his retirement he wrote his memoirs which were published as My Experiences as an Executioner. *Berry performed three executions at Durham.*
Author's collection

first hangman literate enough to write directly about his work. *My Experiences as an Executioner*, was published after his retirement, based on the diaries that he kept during his years of office. It sold at the price of one shilling. Berry destroyed many of the original copies so it has become very rare and, when one is put on the market, now sells for a very high sum. Berry wrote that 'they were more humane in their treatment of the condemned in the North allowing them more privileges than other parts of the country'.

James Billington was born at Farnworth, Lancashire in 1847. He had always wanted to be an executioner and had applied, without success, for Marwood's job but managed to secure the position of executioner for Yorkshire. He eventually took over from James Berry and was in office from 1884–1901. Billington died of bronchitis ten days after his last execution, at Strangeways, Manchester, in December 1901.

James Billington, 1847–1901, held the office of executioner from 1884–1901 and performed two executions at Durham. Author's collection

Chapter 2

Durham Gaol

The present Durham gaol was built at Elvet in 1810 to replace the old prison in the Great North Gate. A sum of £2,000 was pledged towards the cost by Shute Barrington, last but one of the Prince Bishops, who presided from 1791 to 1826. The foundation stone was laid on 31 July 1809 by Sir Henry Vane Tempest. The first architect was sacked, the second died and the building was eventually completed by Ignatius Bonomi. The first prisoners were incarcerated in the new building in 1819.

Until 1816 executions took place at Dryburn, within the grounds of the present Dryburn Hospital. The name Dryburn, or dry burn, is supposed to stem from a time when a Jesuit priest was executed at the spot where a stream once flowed. Legend has it that after the priest's death the stream dried up never to flow again. The place of execution was moved in 1816 to the steps outside the courthouse. A temporary gallows was erected for each hanging.

The Murder Act (1752) allowed bodies of executed criminals to be given to the surgeons for dissection which was a further indignity for the condemned person and their family. Body-snatchers were digging up fresh bodies and selling them to the surgeons for anatomical research. This, of course, caused great distress to the families of the deceased. The act was passed primarily to try and stop the gruesome trade but there were still not enough bodies to satisfy the need for medical research. Body-snatching continued until well into Victorian times. Eventually the law changed and most of the bodies of executed criminals were buried in unmarked graves within the confines of the prison where they were hanged. The bodies were sprinkled with quicklime to speed up decomposition. In 1990, when work was being carried out inside the confines of Durham gaol, remains of some of the executed felons were disturbed. They were removed and later cremated.

Between 1800 and 1899 forty-two men and three women were hanged at Durham. The last public execution here was carried out by Thomas Askern on 16 March 1865 when Matthew Atkinson was hanged for beating his wife to death at Winlaton. For private executions a gallows was set up inside one of the prison yards. All that

A sketch of Durham Old Gaol in Great North Gate which was replaced by the present building in 1810. Author's collection

could then be seen by the public would be the black flag being hoisted and a notice posted on the gate when the execution had been completed.

Sketches and news reports of the early public executions survive to show what these grisly events were like. The day would often be

A view of the road through Framwellgate which led to Framwellgate Moor where many of the early executions took place. Author's collection

declared a public holiday. Throngs of people would gather to watch. Gentlemen would be standing beside stable boys and ladies of quality beside chambermaids. The noise of shrieking and chanting would be deafening. When the condemned person reached the gallows and the noose was put in place a hush would begin to fall throughout the

The condemned cell where a prisoner would be pinioned before being led to his or her execution. Author's collection

A view over the wall of one of the buildings within the confines of Durham Gaol.
The author

crowd of onlookers. As the executioner worked the lever and the rope tightened to do its work complete silence would take over from the hubbub of noise only a few minutes earlier. The silence of the crowd, in all but a few cases, would not be in respect for a death but in expectation of entertainment, morbid curiosity and the dubious thrill of watching a fellow human being die in this way. Many would then head for the drinking dens and spend the remainder of their day's holiday consuming large amounts of alcohol and celebrating the fact that they were alive to do so.

CHAPTER 3

No Motive
1745

O n Friday 21 May 1745, when Thomas Alder, a farmer, was walking in his fields at Hilton Park House, a Sunderland keelman, Nicholas Haddock, brutally attacked him, cutting his throat from ear to ear and, once dead, ripped open his belly and performed other atrocities upon his lifeless body. A young man, one of the farm servants, was passing the field carrying milk for the master's breakfast. Hearing a commotion he put the milk down and walked towards the noise. When he saw what was taking place he froze in utter disbelief. Haddock spotted the servant watching him and threatened to kill the lad also. The young man managed to find his feet, turn and run to Sunderland to procure help. When he led a group of men back to the scene Haddock was standing by the body of

The town of Sunderland where Thomas Alder was brutally murdered by Nicholas Haddock in a field at nearby Hilton Park House. Author's collection

his victim. On seeing the men approach he threatened to kill anyone who came near him. The quick-thinking servant picked up and threw a stone which hit Haddock and knocked him to the ground allowing the others in the group to overpower and secure him.

At his trial Haddock stated that he had never met Alder, in fact, he had never laid eyes on him before that day. He could give no reason for his actions except that he was 'distracted'. He was found guilty of wilful murder and hanged at Durham on Thursday 26 August 1745.

CHAPTER 4

The Disgraced Soldier
1768

On Friday 17 June 1768 Mr Easterby and his servant were riding home to Farrington Hall, near Houghton-le-Spring, from Sunderland. They were stopped near the turnpike by four soldiers whereupon one robbed them of £1.5s (£1.25). The servant managed to strike the soldier inflicting a wound to his head. The servant was then knocked off his horse and Easterby was stabbed with a bayonet several times. Luckily the gentleman was attired in a thick frockcoat so the wounds he received were not life threatening. When the soldiers left the servant recovered himself and went to Sunderland to report what had taken place.

On a thorough search of the soldier's quarters it was found one man was absent. When he eventually returned he was found to be bleeding from a head wound and so was immediately arrested and interrogated severely by an officer. The soldier confessed and also

A mid-twentieth century view of Houghton-le-Spring. Author's collection

gave up the names of his three accomplices. The four men, John Slaid, George Forster, John Adams and Thomas Croaker were all given a harsh flogging before being handed over to the civil power to be tried for highway robbery.

At their trial Forster and Croaker were reprieved and Slaid and Adams sentenced to death. Adams received a reprieve just before the execution was to take place. John Slaid was hanged on Friday 12 August 1768.

CHAPTER 5

The Highwayman
1770

Miss Margaret Banson was the wealthy sister of the writing-master to the Free Grammar School in Newcastle and, as such, she was well respected. At about 9 pm on Monday 6 August 1770 she was returning home in a post-chaise from Durham across Gateshead Fell when a highwayman brandishing a pistol forced the driver to stop on pain of death. He demanded that Margaret hand over her money but she was not a woman easily frightened. She told him she had nothing that was worth his while taking as she had been to Durham on business and had but half a guinea and a few half pennies left on her person. The man took the half-guinea and then demanded a watch but she said she did not have one. Margaret noticed that the man was not comfortably seated on his horse,

The Free Grammar School in Newcastle where Margaret Banson's brother was the writing master in 1770. Author's collection

appeared to be extremely nervous and was not wearing boots or a heavy coat, even though it was a cold evening.

After the event the post-chaise carried on and, about a mile or so further along, met the postman carrying the mail from Newcastle to Durham. They told the postman of what had taken place and advised him to return to Newcastle or get a guard as the thief would still be on the road looking for a likely victim. The postman ignored the advice but did ask at the turnpike for a pistol but none was available. A little way along his route he was joined by a stranger whom he took to be a countryman on his way back from market. As they rode together the postman told the stranger of what had taken place and that he had tried to get a pistol but had been unable to do so. Eventually the stranger stopped the postman and told him in a soft voice that he must hand over his bags. Thinking it was a joke the postman just laughed until the stranger showed a pistol and forced him to alight from his horse and throw the bags on the ground. The postman was then told to get back on his horse and ride on without looking back or he would have his brains blown out.

Both Miss Banson and the postman were able to give a good description of the robber and his horse to the authorities and the following day a man, accompanied by a young woman, was arrested in Newcastle. He gave his name as Robert Hazlitt and said he had been a clerk to Samuel Bamford of Phillip Lane in London. He eventually admitted to robbing the post-chaise but denied stealing the mail bags. He stated that he had an accomplice who had been the one to rob the postman and the mail had been divided between them. Many letters and bills were recovered from a chest which the young woman had in her possession.

On Thursday 16 August, Robert Hazlitt, whose real name was William Hudson, went on trial before Sir John Fielding. Unfortunately for the prisoner Fielding was from London and had been robbed by a highwayman a few months previously and recognised that same thief sitting in the dock opposite him. The jury found Hazlitt guilty of the robbery of Margaret Banson. He still insisted that he had an accomplice whose name was Hewitt. This was investigated and it was found that the man he was accusing was in London at the time of the robberies so could not have been a co-conspirator. It was discovered that Hazlitt had left London in a hurry and had travelled to the north by sea and then had hired a horse at North Shields. He faced a second trial for the robbery of the Newcastle mail for which he was also found guilty. It must have given Fielding great satisfaction to pronounce the sentence of death.

An artist's impression of a highwayman. Author's collection

Whilst he was waiting for his sentence to be carried out the highwayman sent a £20 note and a bill of £14 to Fielding which he had kept hidden in his jacket sleeve. He also told the authorities that the rest of the mail was hidden in a cornfield from where it was duly recovered.

This penitence may have eased his conscious but if he thought it would earn him a reprieve he was sadly mistaken as it neither prevented his execution or what followed. Stealing from the mail was considered an extremely serious crime. On Tuesday 18 September 1770 Hazlitt was hanged on Framwellgate Moor, Durham. After staying suspended for about two hours his body was cut down and taken on a cart to a place near to where the robberies had been carried out. A gibbet of twenty-five feet (7.62 m) in height had been erected on the east side of the road on Gateshead Fell. To this Hazlitt was drawn up to hang in chains as a warning and gruesome deterrent to any who might think about carrying out a similar crime.

When the crowd of onlookers had drifted away a frail, elderly man was seen to arrive and kneel before the gibbet. He returned and carried out the same ritual for several days regardless of the weather. One day he prostrated himself on the ground for about an hour but when he tried to rise he appeared unable to do so until he was assisted by some passers by. He told his helpers that he was now easy and then left not to be seen again. It was thought that the old man must have been Hazlitt's father.

It was later reported that, although sentence of death had been passed on Hazlitt, there had been no order by the court for him to be gibbeted in chains.

CHAPTER 6

The Poisoned Cake
1798

In 1798 it would have been extremely difficult for a young girl who was an orphan and illiterate to obtain any kind of employment. Mary Nicholson must have jumped for joy when she was offered a position as a servant at Little Stainton in the house of John Atkinson. Sadly, it seems that if she had felt relief and happiness at finding work it was to be short-lived as her employment appeared to carry duties that she did not expect. It was all too common for a master to take advantage of his female servants as he would know that often leaving his household without any sort of a reference and nowhere to go was not an option for the poorer classes. It is not known exactly what took place to cause Mary to resort to such extreme measures but it is extremely likely she was sexually abused by her master.

It was about 9 pm when Mr Ord, who lived at Newtown near Little Stainton, answered a knock on his door. Standing on the doorstep was a young, bedraggled looking girl who begged him for a bed for the night saying she was lost and very cold. Mr Ord did not consider the waif a threat and, being of a kind nature, did as he was asked. When the events that led up to that night came to light perhaps Mr Ord would have thought he would not be so welcoming to a stranger in the future.

A few weeks previously Mary had gone to Darlington and purchased a small quantity of arsenic from an apothecary. She had taken it back to the Atkinson's kitchen and mixed it with some flour which she knew was to be used to make a pudding for her master. He was away on business at that time but was expected back later that afternoon. Elizabeth Atkinson, John's elderly mother, came into the kitchen soon after and prepared the pudding. The master was late in returning and told his mother that he was not hungry as he had already eaten. Elizabeth, so as not to waste the ingredients, mixed the pudding with a few spices and baked it into a large cake. The cake was then enjoyed by everyone in the household except for the master and, of course, Mary. Within a short time all those who had eaten the

The idyllic village of Stainton in 2006. The residents would not have found it so peaceful in 1798 when Mary Nicholson poisoned her mistress, Elizabeth Atkinson, with arsenic. The author

cake were suffering the effects of the poison but all, except Elizabeth, soon recovered under the ministrations of a doctor. Elizabeth might have received a larger proportion of the arsenic or it may have been because she was elderly and could not fight the effects that she lingered for a few weeks before dying in great pain.

Perhaps the master had a guilty conscience and was worried that Mary could cause him embarrassment or maybe he genuinely had sympathy for the girl. Having no doubt that his mother's death was Mary's doing, instead of reporting the events to the proper sources he told her to leave and that if she returned he would inform the police. It is unclear whether she meant to kill her master or just make him unwell but it is unlikely that she would have understood the fatal effect the poison would have. Mary had wandered around alone and destitute for a few days before knocking on the door of Mr Ord's house.

Mary was in the depths of despair; with no one to turn to for help she left the Ord's house and returned to Little Stainton and told her master that he could send her to gaol or do as he wished because she had nowhere to go and was in torment over the terrible thing she had done. Atkinson, true to his promise, then called for the police and had Mary arrested. She was charged with wilful murder and stood

The War Memorial situated in the village of Stainton. The author

trial at the following Assizes. Although she was found guilty there was some unrecorded debate on a point of law and Mary was sent back to Durham gaol to await the verdict on her fate. The unfortunate girl was then used to run errands for the local dignitaries until twelve magistrates came to a decision on the point of law debate and agreed that the death sentence should apply.

Almost twelve months to the day after her trial Mary was placed on a cart and transported to Framwellgate Moor to be hanged. A huge crowd of spectators gathered to watch as the noose was placed around the young girl's neck. The cart was removed and Mary was suspended for a minute or so when, to the distress of all watching, the rope broke and she fell to the ground. Half-strangled and, in what must have been unbelievable agony, the girl lay where she fell for thirty minutes or so while a fresh rope was procured. One report mentions her conversing with those nearest to her. A rope was eventually brought and the process was repeated, on this occasion successfully, with Mary embracing what was, by this time, probably a very welcome death.

CHAPTER 7

The Colliery Watchman
1819

ames Hamilton was employed as a watchman at Newbottle Colliery, in the Parish of Bishopwearmouth, and had a cabin at Nesham Main Colliery staithe for his use while he was on duty. On Sunday 16 May, a newcomer to the area, John King, had called at John Jobling's cottage, which was just a short distance from Hamilton's cabin, and asked if he could wash some clothes and tend to his feet which were sore from walking. Jobling gave him a shirt to wear while his clothes were drying and King sat in the cottage and put poultices on his feet. At about 11 pm Hamilton arrived and told King to come to his cabin as he was keeping Jobling and his family up. The following morning Jobling went to see Hamilton and found him sitting at the table with his head in his hand. On closer inspection he noticed blood on Hamilton's hand that appeared to be from an injury to his head. There was also blood on the floor and Jobling noticed that Hamilton's greatcoat, which usually hung on the wall, was missing. A dirk and pistol that had been on the table the night before were also missing and there was no sign of King. Dr John Braugh Taylor was sent for from Sunderland and when he arrived found the injured man seriously disorientated. He thought that one of the wounds could be fatal so had Hamilton taken to the infirmary. The police were treating the case as robbery and circulated a description of the items that were known to be missing from Hamilton's cabin which included a greatcoat, pistol, dirk and a watch.

The following Thursday Hamilton died and, when examined, his body was found to have a severe wound above the right eye and fractures on the same side of his head extending to the base of the skull. The medical examiners reported that the injuries had been caused by a blunt instrument which alerted the police that they were now hunting a murderer. The colliery village was a small and tight-knit community so the police found no shortage of people willing to give information. The finger of guilt pointed to William Charlton and John King who were ultimately arrested as being involved in Hamilton's death.

At 8 am at the Durham Assizes on Saturday 14 August 1819 King (alias David Henley), aged nineteen, stood trial before Sir George Wood for the robbery and murder of James Hamilton on Sunday 16 May of the same year. Charlton, aged twenty, was also indicted for aiding and abetting.

Hamilton's home was in Sunderland but he used the cabin when he was on duty which was usually from 10 pm to 6 am. He patrolled the area never being far from the cabin door, which was not locked when he was at work.

Giving evidence, Nicholas Wilson, a close acquaintance of Hamilton, stated that he had visited him in his cabin about three weeks before the murder. Charlton was there and told them that he had just returned from Hull where he had been looking for a ship to take him northward. He had asked Hamilton if he could stay in the cabin as he had nowhere to sleep but was told he could not as it was against regulations. Wilson again saw Hamilton in his cabin with King on Sunday 16 May.

Jobling then gave his testimony as to finding the injured man early on the morning of Monday 17 May. His statement was corroborated by his son, Thomas, who had also been present. Next, the doctors who had been involved gave their opinions as to cause of death. They added that a poker would have been a likely weapon.

Francis Emmett lived at Dent's Hole near Newcastle and at about 8 am on Monday had met a man in a neighbour's shop who said he was in great need of money. His story was that he had been shipwrecked off Scarborough and his father had drowned. He asked Emmett if he would buy a pistol. Emmett told him he did not want a pistol so then the man offered him a watch for 30s (£1.50), saying it had belonged to his father. Emmett took the watch to show to a neighbour as he did not know the value of such items and eventually offered the man 10s (50p). This was accepted but, being suspicious of the whole affair, Emmett took the watch to PC George Rutherford who, also thinking the story rather suspect, kept hold of the timepiece. Emmett identified King as the man who had sold him the watch. The shop where Emmett had met the man belonged to Margaret Cram, who also gave testimony to seeing King that morning. He had offered to sell her a greatcoat which she had bought for 8d (4p) to give to her son. When she heard about the robbery and murder she retrieved the greatcoat from her son and took it to the police.

Margaret Heasman, Hamilton's daughter, had seen her father on Sunday night as he was leaving for work. He had put his watch in his pocket and took his pistol and dirk as he always did when he was on

Dent's Hole near Newcastle where John King had sold some of the possessions that he had stolen from James Hamilton. Author's collection

duty. He did not put on his greatcoat which was left hanging on the wall. The watch in police possession was very distinctive as it had the Freemasons' Arms on the dial and Margaret was able to be fairly sure it was the one that had belonged to her father. The greatcoat she was able to identify with absolute certainty.

James Cumming, who was an assistant at the House of Correction at Alnwick, apprehended a man on 19 May who answered the description of a man sought for robbery. King told him his name was David Henley and he had had nothing to do with the robbery but he had bloodstains on his shirt and was in possession of a pistol. On finding the pistol King told his captor it had belonged to his father and related the fictitious story of the shipwreck. John Jobling and William Darling, who also knew King by sight, were sent to Alnwick to identify the prisoner. Jobling not only recognised the man who gave his name as Henley but also the shirt he was wearing as the one he had given King to put on while his washing was drying. King was then transported back to Durham.

John More and Thomas Telford had searched Hamilton's cabin and found his jacket, handkerchief, penknife and a small block of wood all bloodstained. They also found a poker covered in blood. The poker was produced at the trial and the two doctors that had examined the body agreed that it had been a blunt instrument such as this that had inflicted the wounds on Hamilton's face and skull.

Two workmen from Messrs Fenwick and Company's glasshouse stated that King and Charlton had been staying at the caulk house (a place where poor people often slept when they had nowhere else to go) for about three weeks and seemed to have done nothing but loiter about. Charlton agreed that they had slept at the caulk house as, he stated, he was poor and 'had neither meat nor money'. They were last seen there on the 16 May when, after eating together, they left between 9 and 10 pm.

Thomas Glendinning, publican of the Seven Stars in Pandon, Newcastle, stated that on the 17 May Charlton had asked him to look after £2 for him. They had also been seen in the public house by Mary Eddy and Margaret Newton. The two men were in a private room talking quietly and although the women could not hear the full conversation they did hear Charlton say that what was between them the world should never know. When Charlton was taken into custody he had money in his pocket and blood on his shirt. He explained the blood by saying it had come from a sore on his neck. He denied having any part in the robbery and also of being acquainted with King.

The court asked the two prisoners if there was anyone who could speak as to their characters but both men said as they were strangers to this part of the country they knew no one well enough. Both were seamen with King having arrived at Shields on a cutter about a month previously and Charlton having sailed from America to Hull where he had left his ship and travelled north.

King told the court that it was Charlton who had given him the goods to sell and that when he had left the cabin Hamilton had been asleep. This story was not believed and the jury found the two men guilty of wilful murder. After the sentence of death was passed King shouted that he was innocent and that all in the court were a parcel of rogues and villains and he hoped that God Almighty would fall upon them all. As the prisoners left the dock Charlton leaped on King and struck him a violent blow whilst shouting that he had committed two murders, his as well as Hamilton's.

On Sunday, the day before the execution was due to take place, King was in a terrible state, seeming more dead than alive, when he went to chapel to hear a sermon given by Reverend Wheeler and to receive the sacrament. Perhaps the thought of meeting his Maker with a lie and the death of a second victim was more than his conscience could stand. He confessed to Reverend Wheeler that he was guilty of murdering Hamilton and that Charlton had known nothing about it. He had met up with Charlton on the road between Newcastle and

Sunderland after the deed was done. Charlton had gone aboard a Scottish vessel to get a berth but everyone was asleep. He had found a jacket with a pocket book and £5 in it which was how he had come by the money. Charlton shook hands with King and thanked him for telling the truth. Twelve judges were immediately called to give an opinion on King's admission that Charlton was innocent of the murder.

At 9 am on Monday 16 August 1819, at the front of the new gaol in the City of Durham, before a large crowd of spectators, only one man walked to the scaffold. James King's soul was recommended to the mercy of God as the noose was fastened around his neck. His body was afterwards given to the surgeons for dissection.

CHAPTER 8

I 'Will' have your Money
1822

Because the key players in this case both had the name of Robert Peat, to avoid confusion, the younger of the two men will be referred to as 'Robert' and the elder 'Mr Peat'.

Mr Peat and Robert were half-cousins and had once been very close. In 1808 Mr Peat had made a will leaving a legacy to Robert but in 1815, because they had a serious dispute, Mr Peat changed his will leaving everything to his wife. Robert was extremely unhappy with this and did everything in his power to get back into Mr Peat's good books including visiting his house once a week even though he was not made welcome. Robert lived at Ravensworth near Richmond and Mr Peat at Darlington. Mrs Peat always bought her vegetables and meat from Darlington market so Robert made sure he visited their house on the days the market was held, so she would be out. This was

An early view of Richmond where Robert Peat lived with his wife and son in 1822.
Author's collection

probably so he could talk to Mr Peat on his own and try to change his decision. Eventually, when he realised that all his attempts were in vain, he must have decided that if he could not claim the legacy by fair means then he would use foul and his thoughts turned to theft and murder.

On 10 June 1822 he told a neighbour that the old woman 'wanted to wrong him out of the brass' and he was going to watch for her leaving for market and then go and see Mr Peat. Later that same day he showed the same neighbour a bottle of laudanum and said he wished 'the old woman had it and it would do her a trick' and also said that he had managed to get the wills. On the morning of Monday 24 June Robert again visited Mr Peat's house after Mrs Peat had gone to market, leaving a large leg of lamb in a quart of water on the fire to boil. Robert left before the woman returned but kept watch on the house. Mrs Peat went to the market a second time and when she returned Robert followed her inside. He told her he had already visited once that day and then asked if she had read the newspapers because there was an article about someone being poisoned with bad water. Mrs Peat snapped at him, saying she had better things to do than read the newspapers. Mr Peat had gone into the yard and would not come back into the house until Robert had left.

Mr Peat and his wife then sat down to a lunch of broth and lamb which, at the time, they thought had rather a peculiar taste, but food could not be wasted so they cleared their plates. Robert visited the house again at 4 pm where he found the couple violently ill

The Market Place in Darlington where Mrs Peat did her shopping. Author's collection

and vomiting. He stayed within the vicinity and kept looking through the window. A neighbour, Mary Bolam, had gone in to offer help to the old couple and when she saw Robert she asked him to go for a doctor. He refused saying that he did not want Mrs Peat to know he was still in the town but, curiously, he called back to the house at 10 pm and said he would stay the night. Mary advised him to go home telling him there was nothing he could do to help. No doctor was called and later that night Mr Peat died. A little of the lamb had been shared out amongst several of the neighbours and all who had eaten it had become ill but they and Mrs Peat all recovered. The effects had been so violent and the meat had been such a dark colour that poison was immediately suspected and the finger pointed at Robert.

Although suspicion and gossip was rife, for some unrecorded reason, it was to be four weeks after Mr Peat had been buried before Robert was arrested. Prior to his arrest he had gone back to the chemist, John Smith, from whom he had bought the laudanum, and asked if he remembered him, saying that he was suspected of murder but it could not have been him as he still had the drug at home. Smith later gave testimony to this and to the fact that when Robert had purchased the drug he had told the chemist it was for some old ladies at Middleton. A medical man gave evidence that he had given a taste of laudanum to everyone who had eaten the lamb and they all agreed that the lamb had had the same taste. There was no defence offered and many believed that if there had been Robert would have escaped punishment. On the slight evidence that was related he was found guilty and sentenced to death for the wilful murder of seventy-six-year-old Robert Peat.

In an admission of theft Robert wrote to his wife telling her to have his son give up the wills that he had stolen from Mr Peat. He added 'Think no more of me, my chance is very bad.' He was right about his chances being 'bad' as on Friday 9 August 1822, Robert Peat, then aged fifty, walked to the scaffold to be hanged by the neck until he was dead.

CHAPTER 9

Trial of a Servant
1831

T he trial of a nineteen-year-old youth caused a sensation in the town of Durham when the courthouse filled by 8 am with not even standing room remaining. Thomas Clark came before Justice Littledale at Durham Assizes on Friday 25 February 1831 accused of the wilful murder of Mary Ann Westhorpe on Sunday 8 August 1830. The trial began at 9 am and it was after 10 pm when all the witnesses had finally been heard. The judge ordered that the jury remain together overnight and hold no conversation with anyone but themselves regarding anything relating to the subject of the trial. They would reconvene on the following morning at 9 am when the judge would make his summing up speech and the jury would be asked to consider their verdict. The twelve men, accompanied by two officials, were taken to Mrs Best's Half Moon Inn to spend the night.

Hallgarth Mill, near Pittington, where the Oliver family and their servants resided in 1831. Author's collection

Clark and Mary Ann, who was seventeen, had been in service to Stephen Oliver and his wife, a wealthy couple, who lived at Hallgarth Mill near Pittington. Mr and Mrs Oliver had gone out for the day to Durham leaving the servants behind to carry on with their chores. The sight that awaited the master and mistress when they returned that Sunday evening was anything but a welcome one. A crowd of curious neighbours were standing outside their house talking in hushed whispers. On entering their home the Olivers were confronted by the local police constable, Anthony Smith, and Mary's lifeless body lying in pools of her own blood which had gushed from wounds as her skull was bashed in and her throat cut.

Clark had been seen that evening in a field nearby the mill and from there he had headed to Sherburn. As he neared the village he was met by two pitmen whom he told that six men had broken into the house,

An extract from Reid's map showing the location of Pittington, near to Hallgarth Mill, where Thomas Clark murdered Mary Ann Westhorpe in 1831. Author's collection

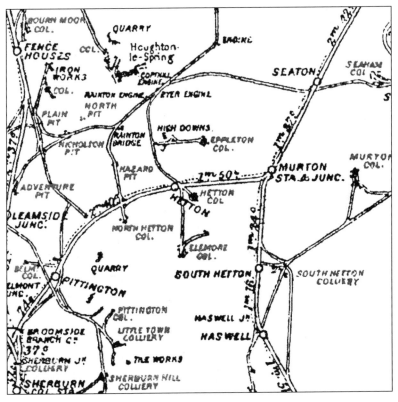

presumably with the intention of robbery, and had attacked him and Mary, whom he feared was dead. When the pitmen, along with PC Smith, followed Clark back to the mill they found Mary's battered and broken body with a bloodstained poker and kitchen knife lying nearby.

Oliver had left a considerable amount of money in a box in the desk which was now gone, so the motive for the crime had been robbery, but by whom? Clark described the six men as having been wearing sailor's garb but, although enquiries were made around the local vicinity, no one else had seen these men anywhere around the area.

Although Clark's clothes had been torn and bloody, he had only a small injury to his head so his version of events appeared suspicious and he was arrested for the murder.

No one knows what really happened that day but after the two-day trial, the summing up suggested that Clark had probably decided to steal the money but had been seen by Mary Ann and he had killed her to keep her quiet and then taken the money to hide in one of the surrounding fields. If his story of the six attackers had been accepted he could have retrieved the money at a later date. The jury decided that Clark had murdered Mary Ann in cold blood with the motive stemming from greed. They brought in a verdict of guilty and he was sentenced to death.

The youth was led to the New Drop in front of the courthouse on Monday 28 February 1831. Reports of the time suggested there was a crowd of some 15,000 people gathered to watch his demise. His final words before the cap was placed over his head and the noose around his neck were: 'Gentleman I die for another man's crimes. I am innocent.' His body, when cut down, was given to the surgeons for dissection.

The Pitman & the Magistrate 1832

The early nineteenth century saw terrible disasters and great loss of life in the mining industry. Miners were employed under what was called a bond system which entailed being contracted to a master for a year at one colliery for a fee, usually one shilling. If a miner broke his bond he could be arrested and either transported or blacklisted. This system worked entirely to the colliery owner's benefit because he did not have to give any guarantee of continuous employment to his bondsmen. The miners were usually paid in vouchers which could only be spent at company shops where exorbitant prices were charged so many were in continuous debt. Also, because they lived in pit cottages owned by the company, any dissent would not only result in dismissal but also eviction. Inevitably the miners rose up against their lot and strikes were staged. There had been a major strike in 1831 and another took place in 1832, turbulent years for everyone involved in the mining industry.

In April 1832 Cuthbert Skipsey, a miners' leader at North Shields, was shot and killed by a constable. The constable received only a six month prison sentence on a recommendation for leniency by the judge. In the next fatal incident to take place that year the sentence was far from lenient.

On 11 June Nicholas Fairles, a seventy-one-year-old well-known local magistrate, was returning home from Gateshead across Jarrow Slake. At the same time two miners, Ralph Armstrong and William Jobling, who were out on strike from Jarrow Colliery, were having a drink in Turner's public house in South Shields. At about 5 pm Fairles reached the toll gate and was stopped by the two miners who begged money from him. Apparently, Fairles had previously been responsible for sending Armstrong's brother to gaol. Whether it was because Fairles refused to respond to the miners' pleas for money or because a grudge was held is not known but Armstrong attacked him with a stone and the two men ran off leaving the victim by the roadside with severe head wounds. The attack had been witnessed by someone in a nearby house so assistance was quickly sought and the

An early view of the Market Place, South Shields. It was nearby where Nicholas Fairless was attacked by William Armstrong and William Jobling in 1832.
Author's collection

badly injured Fairles was taken home. A reward of £300 was offered by the government and £100 by the vestry of St Hilda for information leading to the apprehension of those responsible. These were huge sums of money at that time and Jobling was soon arrested at South Shields. It was thought that Armstrong, who was an ex-seaman, had probably jumped aboard a ship and was long gone. Before being confined in Durham gaol Jobling was taken to Fairles who identified him as one of the men present at the attack but not the man who actually wielded the blows. On 21 June Fairles died of his injuries and his funeral was held on 27 June. It was recorded that a great many high ranking officials attended. The flag on the church steeple and on several ships moored in the harbour were at half mast and most of the shops in the town were closed.

Jobling was charged with murder and his trial was held before Justice Parke at Durham Assizes on Wednesday 1 August. It was a foregone conclusion that Jobling would be found guilty. He was to be made an example of even though he did not actually commit the crime. The politics of the time meant that the miners had to be kept down and what better way to do that than show, in this instance at least, the officials were in control and any form of criminal activity would be dealt with quickly and harshly. As far as the court was

A view of Jarrow Colliery where William Armstrong and William Jobling had been working until the strike in 1832. Author's collection

concerned he was guilty of condoning the murder by watching and then running away and leaving the helpless victim lying where he had fallen. The jury were out for only fifteen minutes before returning a verdict of guilty. Justice Parke, in his summing up, said 'Combinations which are alike injurious to the public interest and to the interests of those persons concerned with them. I trust that death will deter them following your example.' With that said he sentenced Jobling to be hanged and his body to be gibbeted on Jarrow Slake. Even if Armstrong had also been caught and tried it is almost certain that Jobling would still have been hanged alongside him.

Jobling's execution took place on Friday 3 August and Thomas Hepburn, leader of the pitmen's union, asked the miners not to go the execution but to attend a meeting at Boldon Colliery on that day. Perhaps this was to avoid any trouble or because he thought if the miners witnessed the hanging it would cause them to break ranks. Even though the miners were absent from the execution there was still a huge crowd of spectators who all fell silent as the rope was put around Jobling's neck. Then someone in the crowd shouted 'Farewell Jobling' and in a natural reaction the condemned man turned his head towards the sound. This movement displaced the rope slightly and, as a result, instead of a quick death, Jobling slowly strangled.

After the hanging Jobling's body was stripped and covered in pitch. Flat iron bars were riveted together horizontally around him forming a cage. Vertical bars were then attached to stirrups on his feet and encased the sides of his body and head. At the top of his head a ring was attached. His head and face were covered in a white cloth. On Monday 6 August Jobling's body was placed on a four-wheeled cart and taken to Jarrow Slake. In a long procession, organised for maximum impact and protection, Hussars, infantry and officers of the gaol accompanied the cart on its journey. The route took them through Chester-le-Street, Picktree, Sludge Row, Porto Bello, over the Black Fell to White Mare Pool and then along the South Shield turnpike road to their destination. The body was then hoisted onto the gibbet, the construction of which consisted of a thick piece of timber fixed into stone and sunk about five feet (1.75 m) into the ground with iron bars up each side to prevent it being sawn down. The body was suspended from another piece of sturdy timber that projected out about three feet (c.1 m). At high water the tide covered the base but left about seventeen feet (c.5 m) visible. It may have been meant as a grim warning of the punishment meted out for anyone contemplating a similar crime or, in more probability, it was meant as a tactic to demoralise the union and those concerned must have hoped that Jobling's sightless eyes would stare out over the Fell long after the flesh rotted and the bones bleached. Whatever the politics behind the gibbeting, they were thwarted on the dark night of 31 August. For a short time a policeman watched the site but as soon as the body was left unguarded it was removed by persons unknown with the

Winter's Gibbet at Elsdon where William Winter was hung in chains in 1792. It was a construction such as this that would have been used to suspend William Jobling's body after he was executed. Author's collection

whereabouts of his final resting place remaining undiscovered to this day. Jobling was the last person in the north to suffer the indignity of the gibbet.

Jobling's wife, Isabella, could see the gibbet from the cottage in which she lived. She eventually became senile and went into South

Shields workhouse where she died in 1891. The trial and subsequent punishment were immortalized in a ballad which gave Jobling, not what the authorities intended, the role of a martyr:

> *'Farewell Jobling' rang the shout from the crowd*
> *As he was launched into eternity*
> *And on Jarrow Slake Gibbet 21 feet high*
> *He was left to rot in the hot summer sky.*
> *William Jobling, an illiterate man*
> *A scapegoat an innocent victim*
> *An example to the striking miners of the time*
> *Sentenced to hang for another man's crime.*

CHAPTER 11

Murder On Board the *Phoenix* 1839

On the morning of Thursday 13 June 1839 James Alderton, a keelman of Sunderland, was aboard his keel when he noticed something white lying on the river bed. Picking up the pole that was used to move his keel he managed to hook the unidentified object and called to another keelman, Benjamin Howe, and his two sailors to help him. When the four men managed to lift the object on board the keel it was found to be the body of a man. Around the middle of the body a sturdy rope had been tied and then attached to a large, heavy rock. When they took the body to land Sergeant Benjamin Holmes was sent for as this was obviously a murder. The rock proved to weigh about seven stone (c. 45 kg). The man was dressed in a flannel shirt, flannel belt, white linen shirt and stockings. There was a ring on the fourth finger of his left hand. The body was taken to the deadhouse, which was the old workhouse on Monkwearmouth shore, where Dr William John Dodd examined it.

The river at Sunderland where the body of Johann Berkholtz was found. Author's collection

He found the face to be badly disfigured with the left eye completely smashed in. There were two deep wounds to the forehead and the skull was a mass of broken bones. There were bruises to the body and a red mark on the side of the neck. The doctor reported that a blunt instrument, such as a hammer, had been used to inflict the wounds to the face and head and death would have been instantaneous. The red mark on the neck had been caused after death and was perhaps from a piece of folded cloth or a handkerchief.

Sergeant Holmes conducted enquiries to find out the identity of the dead man and it was discovered a captain from one of the vessels berthed at Sunderland was missing. Daniel Pust, a seaman on board the *Phoenix* of Stettin, went to the workhouse and identified the body as that of his captain, Johann Fredrich Berkholtz. On further investigation, Jacob Fredrich Ehlert, the mate aboard the *Phoenix*, was taken into custody charged with the murder of Berkholtz.

Ehlert, who was twenty-eight, stood trial at Durham Assizes on Saturday 7 July before Justice Coltman. As the prisoner could speak no English, Mr Blech, a German interpreter, was brought into court and George Booth, son of the Prussian consul, was also in attendance. Justice Coltman asked the prisoner if he would prefer half of the jury to be made up with his countrymen but the offer was declined. Mr Ingham and Mr Lotherington were counsel for the prosecution and Mr Knowles for the defence.

Daniel Muller was the first and primary witness. He gave his age as nineteen and his employment as an apprentice aboard the *Phoenix*. His version of events was that he went on watch at midnight on Tuesday 11 June and was to be relieved by the cook at 2 am on Wednesday. Ehlert had come to Muller whilst he was still on duty and told him to go with him to the captain's cabin. The youth asked why but Ehlert gave no answer and went into the cabin himself bringing out a bottle of corn brandy. After they had both had a drink Ehlert once again went into the cabin and this time Muller accompanied him. Ehlert had no shoes on and told Muller to take his off, which he did. The cabin was dark and Ehlert was holding a lantern covered with a jacket which he handed to Muller telling him to take the covering off the lantern. Muller did as he was told and, by the light, he saw the captain asleep in his berth. He also noticed that Ehlert was holding a 'macker' in his hand. This was an iron instrument, a little like a hammer, usually used to beat salt fish. To Muller's horror Ehlert held the macker in both hands and delivered three violent blows at the sleeping captain's head. The captain groaned once with the first blow and then he was still. Before Muller could run away

Ehlert had locked the cabin door. He then took a small line, about the thickness of a finger and, tying it around the captain's neck, dragged the body from the berth. The captain was wearing only a flannel and a linen shirt so Ehlert put a pair of stockings and trousers on the body. He made a sort of bag from the sheet that was on the berth and then unlocked the cabin door. Muller had run up the stairs but Ehlert followed him and said if he told anyone of this he would kill him but if he kept quiet he would give him £300. When Muller asked Ehlert where he would get that kind of money he said the captain would have it as he had delivered a cargo of wheat to Leith and had been paid for it.

Ehlert then took the glass from the skylight window of the cabin and, going onto the deck, let down a line from one of the sails. Coming back into the cabin he wrapped the body in the bag made from the sheet, tied the line around it and went back onto the deck and pulled it up. Ehlert then threw the body over the starboard side of the ship keeping hold of the line. Muller was then told to bring the small boat round to that side and Ehlert tied the line to it. They both then climbed into the boat and started to row dragging the body through the water. They stopped rowing while Ehlert went ashore and found a rock which he put in the boat. By this time the sheet that the captain had been wrapped in and the trousers he had been wearing had gone. When in deep water, near to the bridge, Ehlert tied the line to the rock and threw it overboard where it sank taking the body with it. It was almost 2 am by the time they returned to the *Phoenix* and Ehlert told Muller to go to bed and he would keep watch until the cook took over.

At 4 am Ehlert woke Muller and loudly told him that the captain wished to be taken ashore. Then, in a whisper, told him to take the small boat ashore and return. If anyone asked he was to say that he had taken the captain ashore on the north side of the river near the ferry landing. Ehlert reminded Muller that if he did not do exactly as he was told he would be killed. The youth did as he was told and when he returned Ehlert gave him a bottle of wine, a bottle of rum, a bottle of Geneva (gin) and some French and Danish money all of which he hid in his berth. When asked why he did not report the murder to anyone Muller stated that he had seen Ehlert kill a man so knew he was capable of murder and was terrified that he would carry out the threat to kill him too.

Ehlert gave his version of events through the interpreter. His testimony was that Muller, not he, had committed the murder and he had not said anything because he felt compassion towards the youth.

Durham Assize Courts at Old Elvet, where the trial of Jacob Ehlert took place.
The author

His statement was not believed because members of the crew had heard him call Muller at 4 am and tell him that the captain wanted to be taken ashore. The court believed that Muller was not as innocent in the event as he proclaimed to be as there were inconsistencies in his story but it was not thought that he had been responsible for any of the fatal blows delivered to the captain.

The jury was out for only fifteen minutes before returning a verdict of guilty of wilful murder against Ehlert. On Friday 16 August 1839 Jacob Ehlert, still proclaiming that it was Muller who had done the deed, was hanged by Calcraft on the green outside Durham gaol. His body was interred, far from any family and the country of his birth, in an unmarked grave within the precincts of the prison.

CHAPTER 12

The Jarrow Murder 1859

In 1859 John Shaftoe Wilthew, born at Whickham in 1833, had lived with his wife Susannah, at Drewitt's Buildings in Jarrow, for about two years. He had worked as a gate-keeper at Palmer and Brother's shipyard for about five weeks prior to which he had been employed as a storekeeper by Leslie Shipbuilders of Hebburn. Susannah was fifty-one and had borne her husband eleven children, three of whom still lived at home. Two boys, aged twelve and thirteen, slept in the bed with their parents and a daughter, Elizabeth, who was eighteen, slept in the same room on a make-shift bed. To supplement their income Susannah's brother, George Charlton, who worked with Wilthew, lodged with them. The marriage was not a happy one as Wilthew would beat, kick and threaten the life of his wife when he was under the influence of drink.

The village of Whickham in the nineteenth century, the birthplace of John Shaftoe Wilthew in 1833. Author's collection

On Monday 18 July 1859 Charlton and Wilthew had left work at 6 pm and returned home to sit and chat. At about 11 pm Charlton went to bed leaving Wilthew eating his supper while his wife pottered about doing chores. Their daughter, Elizabeth, had been on a steamboat excursion to Blaydon and she returned home at about 11 pm and went to bed about half an hour later.

At 4 am on Tuesday morning Charlton was disturbed by a noise in his room. When he opened his eyes it was to see his sister standing beside his bed in her nightdress with her hands to her throat. On sitting up, Charlton realized that blood was oozing through Susannah's fingers and pouring down her nightdress and on to the floor. By this time the children were awake and Charlton sent one of them to fetch a doctor and alert the neighbours. When Dr Saunders arrived he immediately stitched the wound in Susannah's throat but she died about ten minutes later from loss of blood.

To get to the outside water-closet one had to go through the room Charlton slept in and, while he had been trying to stop the bleeding from Susannah's throat, Wilthew had walked through the room to the water-closet and back again. Charlton shouted to him but he did not reply. While the doctor was attending to his sister Charlton went to find her husband. He was lying on the floor in his bedroom with a gash to his own throat inflicted with a razor which lay a little way off under the bed. Wilthew's self-inflicted wound was not life threatening and, after he had been stitched up by a doctor, he was arrested and taken into custody. Wilthew told his daughter and the neighbours that had come to assist that he thought his wife had been up to no good and he was jealous so had cut her throat. When he was charged with his wife's murder by Sergeant Thomas Salter, Wilthew told him there was a letter in a book on the chimney piece that explained why he had done the deed.

The initial inquest was held at the Railway Inn at Jarrow on Wednesday 20 July with the result that Wilthew was committed to stand trial at Durham Assizes. His case was heard before Baron Watson on Tuesday 26 July where he pleaded not guilty to the charge of murder. The letter he had written relating his jealous thoughts was produced in evidence. It stated that Wilthew had suspected his wife of behaving inappropriately with an Irishman who lodged in the rooms below theirs. He thought that his wife laid two loose bricks in a certain way at the top of the stairs as a signal to her lover. Wilthew had moved the bricks and Susannah had put them back the way they were. He admitted that he had written the letter before he had gone to bed on the Monday night and described how he had lain awake from about

A street in Jarrow in the nineteenth century, as it would have looked when John Shaftoe Wilthew lived there with his wife, Susannah, until 1859. Author's collection

2 am on Tuesday morning thinking about the situation and at 4 am had decided to kill his wife. He had risen from his bed, taken hold of a razor and slashed his wife's throat while she was sleeping. Susannah had woken and staggered into Charlton's room and Wilthew had then cut his own throat in an attempt to end his life before the hangman did.

Elizabeth Wilthew and Charlton stated that although Wilthew had been drinking he was not drunk on the night the murder was committed and neighbours testified as to Wilthew's cruel treatment and jealousy of his wife. He was known as a very bigoted and single minded man who, if fixed with a belief, could not be shaken. No basis for Wilthew suspecting Susannah of infidelity came to light and, in fact, her neighbours hotly denied that there were any grounds for jealousy as she had never been anything other than faithful. Mr Price, Wilthew's defence, tried to put forward a plea of insanity due to a diseased mind but there was no evidence to substantiate this. The prosecution – A Liddell, assisted by Mr Fowler – stated that the findings of the court should be that Wilthew had committed a cold-blooded, premeditated murder for which there could be no plea of defence. The jury agreed and brought in a verdict of 'guilty of wilful murder' and he was sentenced to death.

The scaffold was kept within the gaol and, on the evening prior to the execution, the sections were carried onto the green in front of the courthouse where workman fitted them together. From about 7 am crowds of people began to gather in front of the building jostling each other for the best vantage spot. When Wilthew was in the condemned cell he had expressed contriteness for the disgrace he had brought on his family but, other than that statement, he displayed no emotion whatsoever. It was recorded that he appeared to have nerves of steel as he walked to the scaffold on Thursday 11 August 1859 to be dispatched by Thomas Askern. As Wilthew was dropped the stitches in his throat gave way, with blood reddening the white hood below the neck. To the crowd of about 4,000 spectators it gave the impression of decapitation. In actual fact, the inquest on the body showed that Wilthew had died almost instantaneously of a broken neck.

CHAPTER 13

Dangerously Drunk
1860

Thomas Smith was short but powerfully built and had a rather strange countenance as his face was tinged blue from a gunpowder explosion. He had been employed in various roles since the beginning of his working life including chimney sweep, agricultural labourer and seaman. In the latter years he had worked as a miner in numerous pits around County Durham and, in 1860, was living at Winlaton at the house of Matthew and Eleanor Atkinson along with a co-worker, Edward Armstrong. In a rather strange irony Matthew Atkinson would murder his wife five years later (see Chapter 16). Smith was also known to supplement his income and table by being a very astute poacher, having an excellent knowledge of the surrounding fields and woods. This sideline brought him to the attention of the police on more than one occasion.

On Monday 5 November 1860 Smith and Armstrong had gone to Benwell's public house in Winlaton where they joined a company of men. They were introduced to, amongst others, John Baty, a burly, rather stout man, who worked as a slater and was known by his friends as quiet when sober but very bloody-minded in his opinions when under the influence of drink. Baty lived at Blaydon and had attended a pigeon shooting match at Blaydon Burn before calling into the public house. The two men, along with others of the company, later moved to Parker's beer house where Baty, who was an avid gambler, produced two half sovereigns and two shillings for the purpose of making bets. As no bets were laid the money was returned to Baty's pocket but not before everyone in the company knew it was in his possession. A little after midnight Smith put his arm around Baty and suggested they walk home together. Both men were under the influence of drink with Baty being the worse of the two.

In the very early hours of Tuesday morning two men walking down Blaydon Bank at different times passed what they thought was a man asleep, neither of them stopped to see if they could be of any assistance. George Oakley Nixon, a manufacturer from Winlaton,

The town of Blaydon where John Baty was living until his murder by Thomas Smith in 1860. Author's collection

was also walking home when he met up with the second walker who told him about the man in the ditch. Nixon thought he had better take a closer look in case the man was injured. On getting close to the recumbent figure Nixon realised that he was dead. There was a wound to the man's temple and, although it had been an extremely cold night, the man was wearing only a shirt, drawers, stockings and a neckerchief. Nixon immediately went to inform PC James Kelly of the discovery. Dr Edward Emerson Callender was sent for and when he confirmed that the man was dead the body was conveyed on a cart to the Commercial Inn at Winlaton to await an inquest. Dr Callender examined the body and found a small wound to the cheek and a deep gash to the temple. He could not say for certain that the wound itself had caused death but thought it probable. Superintendent Jabez Squires of the Durham constabulary, along with a body of men, began an investigation. They found a large quantity of blood on a boundary wall a little way from where the body was found. There were two theories as to what had occurred. One was that the wound had been inflicted by a blow at the wall and the other was that he had fallen against the wall and hit his head. It was surmised that the man had then staggered on for a few yards before falling. The soles of his stockings were clean so it appeared that his shoes had been removed after he fell. A coat, waistcoat, shoes and trousers were found in a nearby field and at Knob End woods a small but heavy bludgeon, known as a morgan rattler, was discovered.

With this new evidence another medical examiner, Mr Barkus from Gateshead, who was known to have considerable experience, was asked to inspect the body. His opinion was that the head wound had certainly caused death and had been inflicted with such force that it was unlikely for it to have been caused by the man stumbling against a wall.

It was not long before the dead man was identified as John Baty and it was ascertained that he had last been seen in the company of Smith. It was also found that the shoes and trousers found did not belong to Baty. Because Smith had worked as a seaman it was thought that he may leave the country aboard a ship so the police concentrated their efforts to find him around the nearby ports. The following week he was apprehended at Whitby wearing Baty's shoes and trousers. Smith admitted to the police that he and Baty had had a drunken argument but denied murder.

Smith was committed to take his trial at the Durham Winter Assizes before Justice Keating. The prosecution counsel for the Crown was Mr Seymour who put forward the motive as robbery. The men around the area lived in harsh times and were known to be 'rough', many of them carrying some form of small weapon. Smith was known to always carry a morgan rattler on his person. Baty was so drunk when he left the beer house that he would have been unable to put up much resistance if he were to be attacked. The scenario that was described was a drunken fight, the two men stripping and Smith hitting Baty with the bludgeon with great force, robbing him of money and clothes and then leaving him to die. If Smith was innocent of any crime why had he got rid of his bludgeon and why had he left the area?

The defence counsel, represented by Mr A Liddell, argued for manslaughter rather than murder as the two men were drunk. Witnesses gave evidence to the fact that when the two men had left the public house they were on amicable terms. There could have been no premeditation or grudge as Smith had only met Baty that night. Smith's version of events was that they were having a drunken argument which got out of hand. They stripped to fight and Baty had been thrown against the wall. Smith had then fumbled around in the dark for his clothes, picking up the wrong shoes and trousers. Why would he steal a man's clothes and leave his own behind? If the intent had been robbery then where was the money as Smith had only 1s 6d (7.5p) on his person when he was arrested. The doctor's examination had not been conclusive as to the cause of death so Baty could have died from loss of blood, exposure to the cold or both.

At the last minute Smith withdrew his statement that Baty had fallen against the wall and admitted that he had struck him with the morgan rattler. He had not intended to kill him and had not realised when he left the scene that Baty was seriously injured or in any danger and was horrified to learn that he was dead.

Justice Keating directed the jury to consider all the evidence and if they thought that Smith had not contributed to Baty's death in any way then they must acquit him. If they believed the blow was struck in furtherance of a felonious object, such as robbery, even if the blow had not been intended to kill, then the verdict must be wilful murder. If they believed Smith's statement that he had delivered the blow during a fight with no intention to kill then the verdict must be manslaughter.

The jury retired and, after an absence of two hours, returned to the court and asked for some of the evidence to be repeated. Their request was complied with and they retired once again. An hour later they gave their verdict as 'guilty of wilful murder' and Smith was sentenced to death.

CHAPTER 14

The Jealous Miner
1860

The illegitimate son of Ann, Milner Lockey was born in 1802 and baptised in Hart church. He married Ann Meggeson in 1825 at Brancepeth. The couple had two children, Milner, born in 1833 and Dorothy in 1836, both of them christened in Sedgefield church. Ann Lockey died in October 1856 and was buried at Chester-le-Street. Milner was married a second time, to Elizabeth Wilson, on 5 November 1859 at All Saints' church in Newcastle. The couple lived at Urpeth Colliery with the three children of Elizabeth's previous marriage. This second marriage was destined to last less than a year and in about August 1860 a separation order was issued by Chester-le-Street magistrates. Elizabeth moved, with her three children, to a one-up, one-down cottage beside Urpeth corn mill. Urpeth Mill House was occupied by Thomas Bell. Lockey was an

The Saxon church of St Mary Magdalene at Hart Village where Milner Lockey was baptised in 1802. The author

The church of St Brandon at Brancepeth where Milner Lockey married his first wife, Ann Meggeson, in 1825. Author's collection

extremely jealous man and began accusing his wife of having an affair with Bell but shortly after Elizabeth moved into the cottage the miller went into bankruptcy and had to leave his house.

The bailiff who was sent from the bankruptcy court to sort out Bell's effects was Thomas Harrison, an ex-police inspector from Newcastle, who had been forced to retire when he lost the sight in one of his eyes. Harrison stayed in the miller's house and when all of Bell's belongings and furniture had been disposed of he then had to wait for the crops to be harvested and sold so he moved into Elizabeth's cottage as a lodger. Elizabeth and her children slept upstairs on a mattress and Harrison slept on the bed in the downstairs room. Lockey then began to accuse his wife of having an affair with Harrison. At the later trial it was stated the there appeared to be no foundation to Lockey's jealous ranting, and that this was anything other than a business arrangement for which the money to a woman with three children would have been very welcome.

Lockey visited his wife three times after the separation, the final fatal visit on 29 November 1860. Harrison had not been feeling well that evening and had gone to bed early. Lockey had burst into the cottage and began shouting at his wife. One of Elizabeth's sons, Samuel, was woken by his mother and Lockey arguing and came downstairs. As Samuel crossed the room to get his clothes from where he had left them on a stool Lockey produced a knife and lunged at Elizabeth with the weapon, driving it deep into her thigh. Harrison, who had been sitting on the bed, jumped up to stop him and Lockey turned on him in a savage attack pushing the knife deep into his left side. Harrison staggered to a chair that was beside the bed and there, within minutes, he died. Elizabeth grabbed her husband's wrist and shouted at Samuel to go for help. He ran as fast as he was able to The Ridings, a house about half a mile away, and alerted the occupier, Edward Hart. When the man and boy arrived back at the cottage Lockey and Elizabeth were standing at the door. Hart entered the blood-spattered room and saw Harrison slumped in a chair quite obviously dead. By the time Hart went back outside Lockey had disappeared and Elizabeth, although quite seriously injured, had limped away to get the police. The police arrived in quick time and made a search of the property. The following morning Lockey emerged from a pig-sty where he had lain hidden all night. He was arrested and the initial inquest was held at the Chester-le-Street court where Lockey was committed to trial. He was described as a man of medium height with a muscular build. He had prominent features but his appearance was considered by no means unpleasant.

The church of St Edmund the Bishop at Sedgefield where Milner Lockey's two children were baptised in 1833 and 1836. The author

At the Winter Durham Assizes before Justice Keating with Mr Blackwell and Mr Shield presenting for the Crown and Mr Davison for the defence, Lockey's version of events was that he had visited his wife three times since the separation. On the first occasion he had stayed from about 9 pm until 2 am with them being on amicable terms. About a fortnight later, on a Saturday night, he visited again arriving at about 8 pm. This time Harrison was there and Lockey stated that his wife was not so friendly. When Elizabeth said she was going to bed Lockey followed her upstairs. There was not room for him on the mattress because of the children so he lay on the floor boards. After an hour or so Lockey told her he was cold and uncomfortable and wanted to get into bed so Elizabeth got up and went downstairs allowing him to sleep on the mattress with the children. The following morning Lockey complained that he had travelled nineteen miles and was made to sleep on bare boards when Harrison had a good bed downstairs. Elizabeth told him that her lodger paid for his bed so Lockey retaliated saying he could pay for his as he had a sovereign in his pocket. Elizabeth asked for the sovereign and her husband said she could have it if she would take him back as he only had a fortnight left to stay at the lodgings he was in at that time. Lockey stated that Elizabeth said she would consider it. He stayed a while longer but his wife was talking about Harrison all the time so he left and went to his son's house for his dinner and stayed there until it was time for him to go to work on Monday morning. A week or so later Lockey received a letter from his daughter who lived at Brecondykes. It appears that Dorothy heartily disliked her stepmother and certainly believed that her father had only been married for his money. The contents of her letter must have fuelled the jealous fire that was already burning in Lockey's mind. Dated 23 September 1860, it read as follows:

Dear Father, this comes with my kind love to you, hoping to find you well as it leaves me at present, thank God for it. I write to inform you that your wife has been busy at Brecondykes, and laid you out for everything that was bad – that you offered her a sovereign if she would let you come back and live with her again – and she told you she would not. She was at Pelton that day you went away and was as drunk as a pig. If you will take my advice you will never come where she is again till you are forced to it; but you can please yourself as everyone is talking about what a fool you are. Last time she was at Brecondykes she told them that you had been saying what a fool you were to marry such a woman; that you said she was living with another man; and that she threw a glass of ale at you;

and what a fool she was at not putting such a man as you into gaol as you were such a bad 'un. It is only your money she wants and to do as she likes.

Dorothy Lockey.

Lockey stated that he brooded over the information in the letter, especially after the way he felt he had been badly treated by his wife on his previous visit, and eventually decided to go and see Elizabeth about it. When he arrived at the cottage he had found his wife lying on the bed with Harrison and that was when he felt murder in his heart and used the knife.

Elizabeth, still very weak from her injury and the shock, gave her evidence. She admitted that she had asked for the sovereign but had told her husband she would not have him back. She also adamantly denied that there had been anything going on between her and Harrison and that she had been lying on the bed with him when her husband had visited her. A pitman who worked alongside Lockey at Leasingthorne Colliery also gave evidence to the fact that he had on several occasions heard Lockey make threats towards his wife and would say that if Elizabeth would not live with him then she would not live with anyone else. Another pitman was in court to give similar evidence but he was not called.

A copy of the death certificate issued for Milner Lockey after his execution on 8 February 1860. The informant was William Green, Governor of Durham Gaol.
Courtesy of Peter and Margaret Fox

HC 664099

| | CERTIFIED COPY of an | | | | ENTRY OF DEATH | | | |
| | Pursuant to the Births and | | | | Deaths Registration Act 1953 | | | |

	Registration District			Durham Central				
1860 .	Death in the Sub-district of			Saint Oswald	in the	County of Durham		
Columns:-	1	2	3	4	5	6	7	8	9
No.	When and where died	Name and surname	Sex	Age	Occupation	Cause of death	Signature, description, and residence of informant	When registered	Signature of registrar
371	Twenty Seventh December 1860 County Gaol Elvet Durham	Milner LOCKEY	Male	58	Coal. Miner	Executed for the murder of Thomas HARRISON	William Green Governor of the County Gaol Elvet Durham Present at the death	Twenty eighth December 1860	Thomas Clasp Registrar.

The summing up by the defence was that Lockey had found his wife in an adulterous situation and he had attacked his victims in a fit of passion so therefore the charge should be manslaughter. The prosecution stated that there were absolutely no proven grounds for Lockey's jealousy and that he had lied when he said that his wife and Harrison were in bed together. Samuel, Elizabeth's son, had given testimony that his mother was fully dressed when she was attacked and cuts in the material of her clothing proved this as being fact. An ironmonger had testified that, on the morning of the day of the murder, he had sold a knife to a man he identified as resembling Lockey, which pointed to the attack being premeditated. Mr Blackwell summed up by saying that even if Elizabeth had been in an adulterous affair, there was still no excuse for Lockey's actions. The jury agreed with the prosecution and found the prisoner guilty of wilful murder and attempted murder. As sentence of death was passed Lockey's face was impassive but his fingers belied his calm as he twisted his black worsted cap which he held in his hands before him. On Thursday 27 December 1860 two miners, fifty-eight-year-old Milner Lockey and thirty-five-year-old Thomas Smith, were hanged one after the other by Thomas Askern.

CHAPTER 15

The Old Woman of Hobbletrot 1862

The trial of John Cox gave details of a brutal and un-necessary murder purely for gain but whether the man that hanged for the crime was actually guilty appears slightly doubtful. Even at the present time it is not uncommon for elderly people living on their own in obvious comfort to give rise to rumours of hoarded wealth. Ann Halliday who lived at Hobbletrot on the Witton Gilbert road between Sacriston and Plawsworth, had the bad luck to be one such person. Ann's husband, William, was a butcher by trade and had formerly been the publican of the Shoulder of Mutton in Chester-le-Street. His businesses had been lucrative and the couple had been well off. Ann, however, had a drink problem and, due to this, the couple separated. William, although he could not live with

Chester-le-Street where William Halliday had been publican of the Shoulder of Mutton *in the nineteenth century.* Author's collection

her, must have loved his wife dearly. He had procured the cottage that she lived in and had looked after her generously for many years. There was another small cottage next door to Ann which housed an Irish family, John and Mary Cox and their young child, who had moved there from Felton in about June of 1862. Ann's husband, William, lived not too far distant in a house called Broadmires. As her years advanced Ann eventually overcame her intemperate habits and began socialising with her neighbours and joining in group events. Ann had been born in November 1779 so had reached the age of eighty-three by 1862. On Saturday evening, 2 August of that year, she had attended a tea party at a neighbours, leaving for home before darkness fell.

On Sunday 3 August at about 3 am William Halliday was woken by a loud knocking on his door. On looking out of his window he saw Mary, Ann's next door neighbour, looking up at him. Asking her what she wanted, her reply was that the old woman up the road was 'very bad'. William woke his housekeeper, Mrs Reed, and asked her to go with Mary to see what the problem was. Mrs Reed was getting on in years and did not want to go by herself so she roused a neighbour, Ann Corby, to accompany her and the two women followed Mary to Ann's cottage. Cox was standing at the open door, his shirt and trousers bloodstained. On the women entering they found Ann lying on the floor barely alive and slipping in and out of consciousness mumbling incoherently. A deep wound could be seen on her head and her nightclothes were stained with blood. They managed to lift the frail old woman onto the bed where she muttered 'Oh these Irish.' Ann Corby, meanwhile, had noticed that Mary, rather curiously, was wearing Ann's shawl. The police were sent for and PC Christon took Cox over to the bed and asked Ann if this was the person who had attacked her. Ann's lips moved in what PC Christon construed as a 'yes'. Dr McCabe arrived from Witton Gilbert at about 6.30 am but Ann died a few minutes later. Shortly afterwards, Dr Hudson of Chester-le-Street attended but the two medical men could do nothing except have the body removed for a post-mortem.

The examination of the body revealed horrific injuries which would have caused great pain even on one much younger and fitter than Ann. Fingernail marks on the back pointed to strangulation being attempted; the left arm was broken above the elbow; a heavy blow had been dealt to the jugular vein; a severe wound was on the left temple; four ribs were broken as if been jumped on and the whole body was a mass of bruises and lacerations. The actual cause of death was the wound to the head which was found to have been caused by the point of a coal rake being driven into the temple.

The police made a thorough search of the small cottage and although Ann had suffered an extremely violent death there was very little sign of there having been any struggle. There was a loft to the cottage which had a small window that once had four small panes of glass but was now covered with small boards but there were no signs of these being tampered with. Ann had slept, cooked and relaxed in the room on the ground floor. There was hardly any blood on the floor just a few small spatters where she had been lying when the women had entered. A large stain marked one of the curtains and it was assumed that Ann had grabbed the curtain with her bloodstained hand. Under the bed was a chemise which was soaking wet as if it had been washed. Her bed was made and yet her candlestick was positioned as if she had retired for the night. A small mahogany chest showed signs of having been ransacked and at the end of the bed stood a large chest which would have held linen but this was completely empty. The conclusion was that the murderer or murderers had used the linen to clean the cottage and then disposed of it. The door had been jemmied open but what the police found utterly baffling was that there was no sign of the door key anywhere.

The Coxes were taken into custody and their child placed in the workhouse until Mary's brother could collect him. The couple's story of the sequence of events was that in the early hours of the morning Cox had heard Ann moaning. He had gone to her door and, finding it locked, had prised it open with a poker and entered to find her on the floor. The blood that marked his clothes was from him trying to assist the injured woman. When he realised there was nothing he could do Cox had gone next door for his wife and, after showing her what had occurred, told her to go and fetch William Halliday. He had then returned to Ann's cottage and, going inside, had bolted the door and waited until he had heard the women approaching. Cox insisted that someone must have broken in through the loft to rob and murder the old woman. Mary's version of what had occurred was that Ann had taken a fit and fallen out of bed, thus causing the injuries. On being asked why she was wearing Ann's shawl Mary said that her husband had taken her into Ann's cottage to show her what had happened and then asked her to go for help. Without thinking, she had picked up the shawl and thrown it around her shoulders as protection against the night chill. While Ann's house was being searched there was also a search made of the Cox's. A large fire was burning in the grate with what looked like the remnants of a piece of cloth in it. It appeared possible that the fire had been kept burning all night as a shovel had been placed against it to fan the flames. The ashes were raked out but the police could find nothing amongst them.

Although all the evidence was circumstantial the Coxes were charged with murder and committed for trial at Durham. The Autumn Assizes had just been completed so the couple remained incarcerated in Durham gaol until Tuesday 12 December when the trial was heard before Justice Keating with Mr Maule acting for the defence. Cox was a miner and had been working at Nettlesworth Colliery until his arrest. The court was packed with Irishmen and miners all present to support their co-worker and countryman.

The prosecution put forward the theory that the Cox's believed that Ann Halliday had been a woman of means and had murdered her in the pursuance of a robbery. The wounds the victim had sustained had been inflicted with great force which pointed to the attacker being male. Either Cox or his wife had knocked on the door and on some pretext or other had managed to get Ann to open the door. Cox had then attacked her, perhaps trying to find out where her money was hidden, and while Ann had been lying on the floor dying, the Coxes had ransacked her bedside drawers, made her bed, used her linen from the chest to clean the floor, afterwards taking it into their cottage and burning it upon the fire. Cox had then prised the door open with a poker to make it look as though the perpetrator had locked the door on his way out and taken the key with him. Great store was set on the fact that Ann had supposedly identified Cox as her attacker and there were witnesses in the form of Mrs Reed and Ann Corby who heard her say 'Oh these Irish.'

The defence argued that every thing Cox had said could be true. It was feasible that he had heard Ann cry out, that he had pried open the door on finding it locked and if he had cradled the dying woman in his arms blood would have marked his clothing. No remnants of linen were found in the ashes of the Coxs' fire and if a piece of cloth had been seen whilst the fire was still burning, well, rags were often thrown onto fires. There was nothing to prove that the fire had been burning all night to destroy evidence. As for Ann's identification, she was barely conscious and was only a few minutes from death. It may well have been an Irishman who carried out the deed, but there were hundreds of Irish families living and working in the near vicinity. The other point that was brought was if the Coxes had carried out the crime would Mary have gone for help and would her husband have waited at the scene?

Justice Keating, at his summing up, directed the jury to decide whether the dying woman's identification along with the other circumstantial evidence was enough to find Cox guilty. If they thought that Ann had not been rational at that time then they must find him not guilty. On the other hand he pointed out that a dying person usually told the truth. If they found Cox guilty of murder they must decide whether his wife was also involved and as guilty as he.

The jury was out for two hours before bringing in a verdict of 'guilty of wilful murder' against Cox and 'guilty as an accomplice to murder' against his wife. Justice Keating donned his black cap and passed down sentence of death and the courtroom erupted into utter chaos. Mary was screeching with a high-pitched sound and she rushed towards her husband. The spectators were banging their feet and shouting that it was a travesty of justice. Worried that there would be an attempt by the Irishmen in the court to try and free the prisoners, warders quickly took hold of Cox and dragged him down the steps from the dock. Eventually order was restored and it was revealed that Mary had told a female warder that she was pregnant. Justice Keating ordered twelve matrons to take Mary into a side room to ascertain if this was true. It was established that she was indeed pregnant so a stay of execution was ordered until after she had given birth. Her sentence was later changed to life in penal servitude.

Mary's brother, who had four children of his own, had taken in her young child and was paid a small weekly sum for doing so. Because of the scandal his family had moved and he decided it was not worth the trip back to Chester-le-Street every week to collect the paltry sum so the child was returned to a workhouse. Mary's second child would have probably also been placed into a workhouse.

Cox was a Catholic and was seen in his final hours by Canon Platt who administered Holy Communion and heard his confession. The cleric reported that Cox's demeanour was of a sincere Christian and that he was penitent of all his sins but had insisted that the murder of Ann Halliday was not one of them. Mary, confined in a nearby cell, became more and more agitated as her husband's time drew near. She repeated over and over again that Johnny was innocent and would not hurt a fly.

Early on the morning of Tuesday 23 December 1862 a crowd had already gathered outside the courthouse. In the dim light the silhouette of the gallows could just be discerned overshadowed by the court buildings. As the wintry sun began to rise the instrument of death became clearer to the silent spectators. In the Catholic church nearby all the lights were on as a Mass was said for the doomed man.

The Catholic Church of St Cuthbert in old Elvet, opposite Durham Gaol. Candles were lit and a mass was said here for John Cox before he was executed in 1862 for the murder of Ann Halliday. The author

As the time drew nearer a man was seen to stand on a box under the horizontal bar of the gallows. When he stepped down it could be seen that he had been putting a stout new rope in place. The watching crowds began to swell, not just miners, farm labourers and the lower criminal classes but also respectable ladies and girls who seemed to have sympathy for the man about to face the rope but, by their conversations, nothing but loathing for his wife who was soon to be a widow and her unborn child fatherless. At about 8.30 am Askern, the executioner, appeared and untied the rope, re-tying it lower and then appearing to check the measurements of the drop. As the Cathedral clock chimed 9 am the prisoner appeared, flanked by his official entourage. Cox's face was ashen white and he appeared to totter rather than walk. His hands were clasped in front of him and his arms pinioned. He ascended the scaffold and looked down towards the silent watchers but his eyes were glazed and it is doubtful whether he saw anything of his surroundings. His lips moved and he was heard to say 'Lord, Jesus have mercy on my soul.' Canon Platt, who had accompanied Cox up to the scaffold, stood as near to the drop as possible and waved a hand towards the crowd and every Catholic present fell to their knees. It took less than a minute for Askern to pinion Cox's legs, pull the hood over his face and then the noose. A guttural noise came from deep within the man but was cut off by the loud thud of the drop opening and all that could be seen was the top of his head swinging from side to side, his body obscured from sight by the drop.

Justice Keating, relating to Ann Halliday's identification of her attacker, had said at the trial that a dying person usually speaks the truth. John Cox went to his death still proclaiming his innocence to both God and man, so was that the truth?

CHAPTER 16

Twice Hanged
1865

Matthew Atkinson lived with his wife, Eleanor and his teen-age nephew, Matthew Swinburn, in New Row in the village of High Spen near Winlaton. Atkinson was employed as a miner in the local colliery and was known as a decent man and a hard worker while Eleanor was a drinker and rather slovenly. The sound of the Atkinsons' quarrelling was commonplace and was ignored by the neighbours until one winter's night in 1865.

On Saturday 17 December Atkinson, Swinburn and another nephew had been to a pigeon shooting match a few miles away and returned home at about 11 pm. Atkinson barely had a foot in the door when an argument erupted with his wife. There had been a neighbour, Thomas Leyburn, in the house talking to Eleanor when Atkinson returned and both he and Swinburn beat a hasty retreat not wanting to be involved. The noise of the couple shouting could be heard up and down the road and then Eleanor was seen to run out of the house. Before she got

The village of Winlaton near High Spen where Matthew Atkinson beat his wife to death in 1865. Author's collection

more than a few steps Atkinson dragged her back in. Those listening became worried when the noise of objects being thrown and Eleanor screaming was heard. Some of the neighbours had gathered around the front of the house and one, Benjamin Hunter, knocked at the door but he was ignored. Someone else tried to open the door and Atkinson was heard shouting that he would shoot the first person who tried to come in. Not knowing what else to do the neighbours just stood about awaiting developments. A few minutes later Atkinson came out and just walked around for about fifteen minutes before re-entering the house saying that he was going to finish the b...d off. There were thumps heard and then moaning and more thumps. All went quiet for a minute or two and then Atkinson came to the door and asked three of the neighbours to come inside because he thought he may have killed his wife. Eleanor was lying dead on the floor with terrible injuries from what had obviously been a vicious beating. The police were sent for and PC Harrison of Winlaton arrived in the early hours of Sunday morning and took Atkinson into custody.

An inquest was held at the Board Inn at High Spen where, after some of the neighbours gave testimony and medical statements were heard, Atkinson was committed to stand trial at the next Durham Assizes for the wilful murder of his wife.

Atkinson stood trial before Justice Mellor on Thursday 2 March with Mr Blackwell and Mr Laycock representing for the Crown and Mr Campbell Forster for the defence. Dr Archibald Meggatt gave evidence as to the injuries sustained by the victim. There was a deep, wide wound on the left temple and the back of her head was almost caved-in. One arm and four fingers were broken and there were numerous other cuts and bruises all over the body. A blood-stained coal-rake and poker had been found at the scene and the doctor stated that these weapons had definitely caused some of the injuries. There was no doubt that Atkinson had killed his wife but, because of her dissipated habits, the defence tried to get the charge reduced to manslaughter. PC Thomas Wood had known Atkinson for a number of years and he gave evidence as to Atkinson's previously unblemished character and spoke of Eleanor being of poor character. Some of the neighbours also spoke up on Atkinson's behalf but to no avail. The jury returned a verdict of wilful murder against forty-three year old Atkinson and the judge passed sentence of death.

Preparations for the execution began early on Wednesday 15 March 1865. In the grey dawn workman could be seen bringing out pieces of the structure that was to form the scaffold. As the day wore on groups of people gathered to watch the progress and then, when becoming bored, dispersed and walked away talking in whispers about the prisoner's life and death. Children played on the green laughing and chasing each other under the scaffold, not understanding the significance of the wooden posts and planks. At about 10 am the executioner, Askern, arrived and, almost immediately, began to supervise the work being carried out. If he noticed the curious and sometimes hateful looks directed at him he gave no inkling.

On Thursday morning crowds began arriving before it was light. There was no room now for the children to play as every available space was filled with people from the lowest to the higher classes. Promptly, at 8 am, the prisoner, his religious advisor, Askern and gaol officials appeared on the scaffold. The doomed man was pinioned, hooded and noosed and the trap lever drawn. Atkinson dropped, as was expected, but disappeared out of sight as the rope snapped. The crowd yelled and cheered although it could not be seen how badly the man was injured. Most believed that a person could not be hanged twice for the same crime so would have cheered because they expected that there would now be a reprieve. Nothing could be seen other than a flurry of activity glimpsed behind the boarding of the scaffold and speculation ran rife as to whether Atkinson was dead or alive, half strangled, bones broken, conscious or unconscious. Twenty-five minutes elapsed before the crowd were stunned into silence by the sight of the chaplain stepping back onto the platform closely followed by the wretched man. Atkinson walked steadily enough but his face was ashen and around his neck there was a blood-red mark. The spectators started to boo and hiss as Askern once again began performing the ritual of pinioning, hooding and putting the noose in place. Because the rope was new and not pliant the knot did not slide down easily and the executioner would have been disconcerted with the cat-calls from the crowd. To the spectators' utter horror, Askern grabbed hold of the rope with his right hand and with his left drew the noose as tightly as possible. This was done so roughly that it pulled Atkinson's head right over his shoulder. As the lever was pulled the noose failed to tighten and slipped up to the back of Atkinson's head so that he was suspended almost totally by his chin. As he dropped he convulsed, his knees bending and straightening, with his body uncontrollably being drawn up and down in spasms. This sickening spectacle went on for a few minutes before death finally took him out of his agony. This was the last public execution to take place at Durham.

Five years previously, Atkinson had stood in the same court where he received sentence of death. He and his wife had been called as witnesses to the movements of Thomas Smith who had lodged with them at that time (see Chapter 13).

CHAPTER 17

Jealousy of a Paramour
1869

On Saturday 27 February 1869 John Dolan, a strong, thick-set thirty-seven-year-old Irishman, stood before Justice Lush at Durham Assizes on trial for his life for taking the life of another. Mr Meynell presented for the prosecution and Mr Greenhow for the defence. Dolan had been living with Catherine Keehan at 49 Union Lane, Sunderland. Two other men, Hugh John Ward and Edward Collins, also lived at the premises as lodgers. Ward had lived in the house for about five weeks and he and Dolan had become quite friendly.

On Tuesday 8 December 1868 the two men had been drinking and later went for a walk together. Later events give rise to the probability that their conversation must have revolved around Catherine and that, coupled with the fact that they were drunk must have fuelled jealousy in Dolan towards his lodger. When the two men returned to the house Dolan gave Catherine 6d (2.5p) to get some beer with which she duly returned. Ward helped himself to a glass and handed one to Dolan which was refused. On querying this unusual behaviour Dolan said he was not a glutton and anyway, he had to go to work in the morning but Ward should just help himself. Ward shrugged his shoulders and handed Catherine a glass which she took. Dolan had been sitting with his head bent forward but when Catherine accepted the beer he began to shake his head from side to side saying 'that will do for me'. He then grabbed hold of her and dragged her to the bedroom and bit her on the breast. Ward asked Dolan to stop and he replied he was not going to hurt Catherine, just put her to bed. The lodger, perhaps wishing to stay neutral and not interfere in the couple's affairs, went back to sit in the kitchen. Dolan then began to beat Catherine and drag her around the bedroom by her hair so she screamed for help. Ward entered the bedroom and asked Dolan what he thought he was doing to which the reply was that he was in his own bedroom and he then released Catherine and attacked Ward. Catherine ran out of the house to get the police leaving the

The town of Sunderland where John Dolan stabbed Hugh John Ward to death in 1869. Author's collection

two men struggling violently. When the police arrived the situation had quietened down so, because they had not witnessed the affray, declined to arrest anyone. Catherine told them that there would be murder done if they left the two men together. Dolan promised that he would go to bed and one of the police officers told Catherine that he would be at the end of the lane if she needed him.

No sooner had the police left than Dolan began rummaging in a box and pulled out a knife. Catherine shouted a warning to Ward and then she climbed out of the window and ran down the lane shouting that murder was being done. The other lodger, Collins, had been asleep throughout the whole proceeding but Catherine's cries had awoken him. As he entered the kitchen Ward was sitting by the fireplace and Dolan just crossing the room with a shoemaker's knife in his hand. Before he could fully comprehend the situation Collins saw Dolan lunge at Ward and stab him ferociously. Collins managed to disarm Dolan and just as he did so Police Constable Thomas Coldwell arrived and took the prisoner into custody. A doctor was sent for but it was too late, Ward had been disembowelled by one of the stab wounds and another had taken out his eye.

The defence asked the jury to consider a verdict of manslaughter but it took the twelve good men less than ten minutes to bring a verdict of guilty of wilful murder. When Dolan had listened to the death sentence being passed he shouted that the witnesses had sworn his life away and that if he had had able counsel this judgement would not be taking place. Justice Lush responded by saying that he had had a most able counsel to which Dolan replied that if he had been allowed to speak for himself the outcome would have been very different. Dolan was still muttering against the law and the participants in his trial as he was manacled and led away by two warders to await his execution which was to take place on 22 March.

CHAPTER 18

Death at Darlington 1869

The February Assizes of 1869 at Durham saw Justice Lush in the unenviable position of holding a second man's life in his hands when John McConville stood before him accused of the murder of Phillip Trainer.

The Albert Hill area of Darlington was cramped and overpopulated with many Irish families in residence, most of the men folk employed in the nearby ironworks. Saturday night around the drinking houses was always a busy time for the local constabulary with heavy drinking men letting off steam after a hard week's labour. The night of 30 January 1869 was no exception and the police had been called out to numerous drunken quarrels. One such incident took place at Costello's beer house when William Young went into the yard to use the water closet. He heard someone following him and moved his head just in time to prevent a bullet hitting him. The police were called and Young told them that the man who had fired the revolver was Thomas Finnegan. A sergeant and two police officers found the gunman at the Havelock Arms but when Finnegan saw the law he tried to pull the revolver from his pocket. Whether he meant to shoot will never be known as the weapon got caught in his clothing giving the police the opportunity to overpower and arrest him. Finnegan was charged and then released. This incident had passed without anyone being hurt but an incident later that night was not to have such a peaceful outcome.

Around midnight the same police officers attended a report that a man had been shot and killed outside the Allan Arms on the corner of Killinghall and Nestfield Streets. On arriving they found the body of a man lying in the road. He had been shot through the left eye and would probably have died instantly. The dead man was Phillip Trainer, an Irishman, who had been employed at the old ironworks of Messrs Barningham. Although there was still a crowd of drinkers hovering about the scene the police could extract very little information as the men appeared to close ranks either to protect one of their own or through fear. The victim's body was removed and the police began a serious enquiry into the events leading up to the young man's death.

One man, James Quinn, was taken into custody on the suspicion that he knew who the perpetrator was. Once he had given the police information he asked to remain in custody until the inquest was over because he would be in fear of his life, especially at Albert Hill. Eventually other witnesses were cajoled into speaking out and enough information was forthcoming for the police to suspect three men. The revolver that Finnegan had fired during the earlier incident was initially thought by the police to be the same one that was used in the murder but this was eventually found not to be so. Finnegan, Thomas Hanlon and John McConville, or 'Gentleman John' as he was known, were arrested. Twenty-three-year-old McConville was taken into custody from his lodgings at Harrogate Hill by PC John Dun on Sunday night. On a search being made, cartridges and a revolver case were found but no firearm. The cartridges matched the one that had killed Trainer. Witness statements suggested that there

An extract from a map showing the Albert Hill area of Darlington where many Irish families were crammed into tiny houses.   Ordnance Survey, Darlington 1898

had been some sort of long standing argument between McConville and Trainer but no one was forthcoming with the reason for the bad feeling or the motive for the murder.

At the initial inquest Hanlon was dismissed through lack of any evidence of involvement in the crime and Finnegan's story was that he was selling his revolver to a friend and had gone into the yard to show him that it was in working order by firing into the air and he had not intended harming or frightening anyone. His story was believed and he was released.

The first witness to be called at McConville's trial was John Harrison, an assistant at Mr Benson's ironmongery, Darlington. He stated that on 20 January a man using the name of James Jackson had come into the shop and asked to buy 100 cartridges for a revolver. The assistant had told the man that he was out of that particular cartridge but would order them in. This was done and the customer collected them a couple of days later. Harrison pointed McConville out as being the customer that had used the name Jackson. The hosts of the Allan Arms, George and Ann Turnbull, told the court that there had been five or six men in their kitchen that fateful night. John McConville and Phillip Trainer were amongst the group. An affray had taken place so they were all told to leave the premises. Trainer, who they knew as a quiet young man, had stayed behind talking to a

The Market Place in Darlington as it would have looked when John McConville shot and killed Phillip Trainer in 1869. Author's collection

man called Burns for about ten minutes. Immediately on him leaving the Turnbull's heard the sound of a gunshot and someone shouting that a man had been murdered.

Quinn's testimony was that it appeared to him that McConville had been spoiling for a fight. He asked him that night if he knew the man called Burns whom he pointed to as being in the room. When Quinn had replied in the affirmative McConville had then asked if Burns was a fighting man and Quinn had again answered 'yes'. McConville replied that Burns could not take on his mate Hanlon as he would be too powerful for him and had then put his hand on his breast pocket and said that he had something that would stop any attack. It was following this conversation that the affray had started. On leaving the premises the scuffle had spilled out onto the street and continued for about ten minutes. Quinn had then seen McConville reach into his breast pocket and, pulling out a revolver, fire into the crowd. The revolver was slipped back into his pocket and McConville disappeared around the corner.

After all the evidence had been heard the jury retired and after about an hour's deliberation returned with a verdict of guilty of wilful murder. Justice Lush expressed that he concurred with the verdict for this brutal crime and handed down the sentence of death. It was reported that neither Dolan nor McConville showed any remorse in the time leading up to the day of their execution.

With the change in the law governing executions this was to be the first at Durham to be held in private. The public would see only the black flag hoisted and a notice placed on the gates as the deed

was done. The only members of the public that were permitted to witness the proceedings were a limited number of the press.

On Monday 22 March 1869 John Dolan and John McConville stood side by side, pinioned, with white caps covering their faces. William Calcraft pulled the lever which sent the two men to their deaths in the name of justice.

The executioner, William Calcraft, who performed the double execution on John Dolan and John McConville in 1869. Author's collection

CHAPTER 19

False Witness?
1873

At the Durham Winter Assizes before Justice Denham four men were indicted for the wilful murder of Joseph Waine, at Spennymoor, on Tuesday 16 November 1872. The four men were thirty-two-year-old Hugh Slane who was brother-in-law to twenty-nine-year-old John Hayes, George Beesley, twenty-seven and Terence Rice who was nineteen.

Joseph Waine lived with his wife, Jane, their son, Isaac, and a recently moved in lodger, Wilson, at Duncombe Street in Spennymoor. Separated by a narrow passageway the house next door was occupied by John Hayes, his wife, son and two lodgers, Beesley and Rice. Jane sold tobacco sundries and on the night of Saturday 16 November 1872 at about 10.30 Slane entered the back kitchen to ask for a box of matches. Jane went through to the front room to fetch

The village of Spennymoor where Joseph Waine was kicked to death by four men in 1872. Slane and Hughes were executed in 1873 and Beesley and Rice incarcerated for life. Author's collection

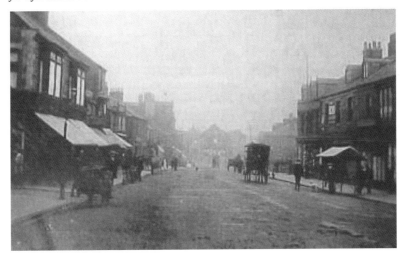

them and when she returned Slane was asking Wilson if he had been at Carrick's Beer House that night as there had been some trouble there earlier. Wilson replied that he had not as he had no money to go out. Slane was drunk and swore at him calling him a liar so Waine intervened and said that Wilson had been in the kitchen with him and his wife all evening. Slane then called Waine a liar and invited him to follow him outside so the issue could be settled. Waine, who had been sitting by the fire filling his pipe, stood up and walked to the front room door but did not go outside. Slane came back in and threw the matches in Waine's face then, grabbing him by the collar, dragged him into the passage between the two houses. Jane followed shouting at Slane to leave her husband alone. Three men that were in Hayes' house had heard the commotion and came to see what was going on. While Slane held the defenceless man down the other three men commenced to kick him. Jane managed to pull one man away from her husband but Hayes pulled her cap and shawl off and threw her out of the passage. Hayes then went back and took a running kick at Waine. The four men then returned to their own house leaving Waine struggling to rise from the floor. Wilson helped him back in and put him on the bed in the front room while Jane went for the police. As she was doing so, two men and Hayes came out of his house and were about to attack her when two men who were passing by stopped them. As Waine was brought back into his house two neighbours, Mary Maughan, who lived nearby in George Street, and Thomas Flynn had called in and Waine asked someone to go for a doctor. Mary went to see Dr O'Hanlon who prescribed salt water and mustard and water to purge Waine's stomach. These did not seem to help the injured man so Mary went back to the doctor and returned with some powders but before these could be administered Waine had died. On Jane's statement to the police five men that were in the Hayes's house were arrested. Jane told the police that the fifth man that had been taken into custody was Wilson, her lodger, and that he had not been involved in the attack so he was released. Wilson then, rather curiously, disappeared from the area although he did leave a written statement relating to the events but this was deemed inadmissible in court. The four men she identified as having been involved were Slane, Hayes, Rice and Beesley.

At the trial, because Waine had not made any statement before he died, the only witnesses to the actual attack were his widow and son. The jury believed their version of events and identification of the men involved, so all four were found guilty and the sentence of death was passed with the date for their execution set for 6 January 1873.

Hayes, Slane and Rice, from their prison cells, made statements that Beesley had not been one of the men involved and a huge effort was made by family and friends to exonerate both Beesley and Rice from the murder. There was a great deal of sympathy for Rice because of his youth. A reprieve was granted while officials looked into the case. It was decided that Beesley and Rice, whilst not being responsible for the murder, had been accessories and their sentences were commuted to life imprisonment. On Monday 13 January 1873 Slane and Hayes walked their last walk to the scaffold to be hanged by Calcraft.

A report in the *Stockton and Cleveland Mercury* in March 1877 showed that efforts were still continuing to have Beesley and Rice completely exonerated and released from gaol. Mr Joseph Rowntree from Leeds, a member of the Society of Friends appeared before the bench at Bishop Auckland Police Court with affidavits for the release of the two men. It was believed by him that perhaps Jane, in all the commotion, had made a mistake with her identification of the parties involved or not seen which of the men had actually attacked her husband. Elizabeth Hayes had not been allowed to give evidence at the trial because she was the wife of one of the accused men but she insisted that Beesley had come in to her house with her son and both had fallen into a drunken sleep at about 7 pm the night of the attack. They had not left the house until the police had taken them into

A view of Bishop Auckland where an appeal was presented to the court by the Society of Friends in 1877 for the release of Beesley and Rice. Author's collection

custody later that night. Both Joseph Hayes junior and a neighbour, Mary Ann Maher, who was also in the house that night, confirmed this evidence. Furthermore, Elizabeth Hayes, Mary Ann Maher and another woman, Margaret Walker, had given signed statements that Rice had been in the house from 6 pm bottling ginger beer and he also did not leave until taken into custody by the police. Perhaps the police did not want to be shown to have made wrongful arrests or perhaps the magistrates did not believe the evidence was reliable. Whatever the legalities of the situation were Beesley and Rice remained incarcerated to complete the sentence the law had dictated.

CHAPTER 20

Arsenic and Carbolic
1873

erhaps the most famous, or infamous, of all the crimes to incur the death penalty during the Victorian era were those carried out by Mary Ann Cotton. Because she was female, a serial killer and the cold calculated nature in which she carried out the murders, the case achieved worldwide notoriety.

Mary Ann Robson was born in October 1832 in Low Moorsley with her brother, Robert, born soon after. Both Mary's parents were very young when they married and, although her father worked as a pitman at East Rainton Colliery, the family's lives would have been one of drudgery and near poverty so there would have been few pleasures for the children. Their father was also deeply religious and extremely strict. The family moved to Murton in County Durham where, when Mary was about thirteen, her father fell down a mine shaft and was killed. A widow left with a young family would usually have to go into a workhouse with her children separated from her. Perhaps this fear looming over Mary Ann's young life was the beginning of her obsession with having money. The awful reality of separation and the workhouse never came to pass as her mother re-married but this did not improve matters for Mary Ann as she and her stepfather had a mutual dislike of each other. At the age of sixteen Mary Ann left home to work as a servant in a large house at South Hetton. It is believed that she was probably a very attractive young lady and certainly innuendoes of loose sexual behaviour were bandied about the village. After about three years, in 1852, Mary Ann left her position as a servant to take an apprenticeship as a dressmaker. Shortly afterwards she married William Mowbray, a miner, by whom she was pregnant.

William and Mary Ann had five children in the first four years of their marriage of which four died. Perhaps because the couple moved around a lot with William taking work wherever he could, or perhaps because there was a high mortality rate for children at that time, there was never any suspicion regarding the deaths of the infants. The couple then had another four children and, with Mary Ann determined

The church of St Peter, Monkwearmouth where Mary Ann Mowbray married George Ward in 1865. Author's collection

never to be poor, after many heated arguments, William took a better paying job aboard the Sunderland steamer *Newburn*. Mary Ann and her five children moved to Sunderland to be near his home port. Three more of the children died of unexplained illnesses before the end of 1864. In January 1865 William injured his foot so returned home to recover but at the end of the month William died suddenly of a gastric disorder. Mary Ann had an insurance policy on her husband's life and, after collecting the money, moved with her remaining children to Seaham Harbour.

Here Mary Ann met Joseph Nattrass who was engaged to another woman. It appears that Mary Ann did all she could to entice him but he would not break off his engagement and he went ahead and married his fiancée. After Joseph's wedding and the burial of yet another child Mary Ann returned to Sunderland, sending her one surviving daughter, Isabella, to live with her mother. She then took employment at Sunderland infirmary where she would clean the wards daily with a mixture of carbolic soap and arsenic.

One of the recovering patients at the infirmary was an engineer, George Ward, with whom Mary Ann struck up a close relationship. When George was discharged from the infirmary he and Mary Ann were married in August 1865 at Monkwearmouth church. Soon after the wedding George became ill and, although a doctor was administering various treatments, he died in October of 1866 at the age of thirty-three. His symptoms were severe gastric pain and paralysis of the limbs. There were accusations against the doctor for the treatment he had given but still no suspicion fell on the bereaved widow.

In November 1866 Mary Ann saw an advertisement for a housekeeper in Pallion. James Robinson, a shipyard foreman, had lost his wife and was looking for someone to look after his house and his four children. Mary Ann applied and was employed. Before Christmas of the same year the youngest of the four children had died of gastric fever. It appears that Robinson, besides needing a home-help, was also in need of someone to console him in his terrible grief and Mary Ann was just the one to do that. Before long she was pregnant with Robinson's child. In March 1867 Mary Ann received word that her mother was very ill so, as a good daughter should, she went to be with her and to visit Isabella the daughter whom she had not seen for nearly two years. By the time Mary Ann arrived her mother was on the mend but a short while later she became ill again and died on the ninth day of Mary Ann's visit. Isabella returned to the Robinson

The twelfth century church of St Andrew in Newcastle. It was here in September 1870 Mary Ann Robinson, using the name Mowbray, married Frederick Cotton.
The author

house with her daughter where, within a month, she and two more of the Robinson children died of a gastric disorder.

Robinson and Mary Ann were married and their daughter, Mary Isabella, was born in November 1867 but was dead by March 1868.

Another daughter was soon born to them but by now, at last, suspicions had begun to creep in. Robinson began to think about the circumstances of the many deaths and the fact that Mary Ann kept on at him to take out insurance on his life and he also found out that she had been running up debt and been selling small items from the house. Eventually he threw Mary Ann out. If Robinson had reported his suspicions to the proper authorities at that time lives would probably have been saved but perhaps he felt a fool for having been taken in by her charming ways or he may have been glad just to be rid of her.

Mary Ann then wandered the streets for a time in the position she had always dreaded. She must have gathered her thoughts together and tried to work out a way of avoiding poverty and the workhouse. Presumably she felt her situation would have been impossible to alter while she had a child in tow. She arrived with her daughter on the doorstep of a female acquaintance asking that she look after the child for a short time. Mary Ann never returned and the child, by this act probably avoiding a painful death, was eventually returned to her father.

By the beginning of 1870 Mary Ann had been introduced to Frederick Cotton who was the brother of her friend Margaret Cotton. Two of Frederick's four children had succumbed to early deaths from typhus and his wife, Adelaide, had recently died of consumption. Since the death of his wife, Margaret had been looking after her brother and his two remaining children, Charles Edward and Frederick junior. In March 1870 Margaret succumbed to an undiagnosed illness leaving the way clear for Mary Ann to console another grief stricken, vulnerable man. In September of 1870 she and Frederick were married at

The only known image to exist of Mary Ann Cotton, looking rather dowdy and not at all like the femme fatal that she was portrayed to be. She was believed to have been responsible for at least twenty deaths by administering poison and was executed in 1873 for the murder of her stepson, Charles Cotton.
Author's collection

St Andrew's in Newcastle, she signing the register as Mary Ann Mowbray. Mary omitted to divulge that she was still married to James Robinson who was very much alive. Her first task as 'Mrs Cotton' appeared to be to insure her husband's and stepson's lives.

Becoming pregnant almost immediately, a son, named Robert Robson Cotton was born in 1871 and soon after Mary Ann heard that Joseph Nattrass was now a widower and was living nearby. Somehow she managed to manoeuvre a move to West Auckland so that she could rekindle the relationship with her ex-lover. The end of 1871 saw the death of her husband from a gastric complaint and Nattrass soon moved in as a lodger. Mary Ann took employment as a nurse to John Quick-Manning who was recovering from smallpox. Quick-Manning was an excise officer and must have seemed a better catch than Nattrass because Mary Ann became his lover and then fell pregnant to him. Perhaps she thought that marriage to her new man was out of the question while she still had Cotton's children and her lodger to take care of. Whatever her reasoning, events began to speed up in her household which led to her downfall.

On 23 March of 1872 Robert Robson died aged just fourteen months. Frederick Cotton, aged ten, followed him on 31 March. Mary Ann was later reported to have said that she would wait to bury Frederick as Nattrass was also very ill and she would handle both burials together. Joseph Nattrass died on 1 April at the age of thirty-nine.

Perhaps these deaths would have also been put down to a contagious gastric fever but for Mary Ann bringing suspicion on herself with a chance remark during a conversation. Mary Ann had tried to put Charles into a workhouse so she could go back to work but had been refused unless she accompanied him. The assistant overseer of the workhouse, Thomas Riley, had asked if she were going to marry Mr Quick-Manning and she answered that she might. Mary Ann had then added that she would not be troubled much longer by her stepson as he was sure to go the way the rest of his family. She added that 'He won't get up.' The remark, at the time, Riley took to mean that Charles would not reach adulthood because the whole family had been sickly. Seven-year-old Charles Edward Cotton died in July of 1872 and when Riley heard of the child's death it put a more sinister light on the conversation he had had with Mary Ann a week previously. He went to the police and told them of Mary Ann's remarks. Riley also spoke to the doctor and asked him not to issue a death certificate until investigations were carried out. Mary Ann had already been to the insurance office to collect on Charles's policy but had been told she would have to have the death certificate before she could collect the money.

A post-mortem was ordered but, even though there was external bruising to the body, death from natural causes was the verdict at the inquest. The newspapers had now picked up on the story and there was a media frenzy of reports relating the items of gossip which were circulating alluding to Mary Ann being a poisoner. Meanwhile a pathologist, Dr Kilburn, who had reservations about the findings of the post-mortem, had taken some of the child's internal organs home. He stored the items until after the inquest when he carried out tests and found that there was arsenic present. On reporting his findings to the authorities the bodies of Joseph Nattrass, Frederick Cotton and Robert Robson were exhumed and all were found to contain arsenic in the stomach and some of the vital organs. Arsenic poisoning would bring about an undignified and agonising death with the symptoms including diarrhoea, vomiting, stomach cramps, excessive sweating and seizures.

Because Mary Ann was pregnant the initial trials were delayed until she gave birth and was strong enough to stand trial. Her daughter was born on 10 January 1873 in Durham gaol and the committal trials on four suspected murders were held in early March at the

A view of Front Street in the village of West Auckland depicting Mary Ann Cotton's house and the Rose and Crown Inn next door. It was in this public house that the committal inquests were held into the accusations of murder.
Author's collection

One of the many rather sensational publications that were produced during Mary Ann Cotton's trial in 1873. Author's collection

Rose and Crown at West Auckland, which was next door to the house she lived in. Although it was suspected that forty-year-old Mary Ann had been instrumental in many murders the authorities decided against further exhumations and she was committed for trial at Durham Assizes charged with only the one murder, that of Charles Edward Cotton.

Charles Russell QC, Mr Greenhow, Mr G Bruce and Mr Trotter prosecuted with Mr Campbell Foster and Mr Part having the unenviable task of presenting the defence. Witness after witness came forward to testify against Mary Ann. They spoke of her cruelty to her stepson before he became ill, the fact that she tended the sick herself with only the occasional visit from the baffled medical men and her seemingly callous attitude towards the deaths. It was proved that she had had arsenic in her possession. Her defence tried to prove that the child had inhaled the arsenic from the wallpaper in the house and from where it had been used, along with carbolic soap, to clean the bed and floor. This was disputed because the large amount of the poison that was present in the child's stomach would have to have been swallowed. After all the evidence had been heard it took the jury just ninety minutes to return their verdict of guilty to Justice Archibald who then pronounced sentence of death. At least Mary Ann's last child would have a chance of reaching adulthood as she was taken from her mother and given to a couple for adoption.

On Saturday 29 March 1873 Mary Ann Cotton walked to the scaffold to be hanged. The executioner was seventy-three-year-old William Calcraft, assisted by George Smith. Calcraft's co-ordination and 'short drop' weight measurements had always left something to be desired so, instead of a quick, clean death, Mary Ann's body twisted and struggled as she was strangled for two or three minutes before finally entering the dark world where, it was believed, she had sent so many others.

Three husbands, her own mother, Joseph Nattrass, Margaret Cotton, five stepchildren and ten of her own children were known to have died of virtually the same symptoms and all had been nursed by Mary Ann. If these events had taken place in the present time this cold and calculating woman who dispatched people as if they were bugs underfoot would have been incarcerated in a prison for the criminally insane and her name would be whispered along with those of the Yorkshire Ripper, Peter Sutcliffe and Harold Shipman.

After Mary Ann's death children, probably with no concept of the significance, would skip rope and play hopscotch to the rhyme:

Mary Ann Cotton, she's dead and forgotten
She lies in a grave with her bones all rotten:
Sing, sing what shall we sing?
Mary Ann Cotton's tied up with string.
Where, where? Up in the air
Sellin black puddens a penny a pair
Mary Ann Cotton dead and she's rotten
She lies in her bed with her eyes wide open
Sing, sing, oh what can I sing?
Mary Ann Cotton is tied up with string
Where, where? Up in the air
Sellin black puddens a penny a pair.

CHAPTER 21

Three Murder Trials
1874

I Stabbed to Death

The 1873/4 Winter Assizes included a particularly busy agenda for Justice Honeyman with three men accused of murder standing trial for their lives. The first of these was Edward Gough, a twenty-two-year-old labourer, living at Sunnyside near Chester-le-Street. On the evening of Monday 7 July 1873 he and James Partridge had been doing some heavy drinking at Livingstone's Beer House at Sunnyside. The two men began to argue and at about 9 pm Gough left the premises but returned shortly afterwards and the quarrel recommenced becoming more and more heated. Eventually the landlord told them he would not tolerate such behaviour on his premises and if they did not quieten down they would have to leave. Gough went outside but, once again, after a short time, returned. He started shouting at Partridge to come with him so he could give him 'what

The village of Sunnyside where Edward Gough stabbed James Partridge in 1874.
Author's collection

for'. The two men then went out by the rear door into the yard with others that were in the room following to watch the inevitable drink-fuelled fight.

According to the many witnesses who gave evidence at the trial Partridge had tried to ignore the taunts both inside and outside the beer house but Gough would not be satisfied until they fought. The two men began to remove their coats but Partridge's arm became stuck which rendered him almost helpless. Gough, having taken off his coat, seized on the opportunity and jumped at his adversary and appeared to strike at him with great force. Partridge stood swaying for a few moments and, to the horror of the onlookers, blood could be seen pouring down his legs and into his shoes. The injured man then fell straight back onto the ground still bleeding profusely from a wound in his thigh. Gough was restrained by some of the men that were present until the police arrived. A bloodstained knife was removed from his person and he was taken into custody. By that time Partridge had bled to death from a stab wound which had severed the femoral artery.

If a murder trial could be called straight forward then this particular case was just that. There was no question of Gough not being guilty and that was the verdict of the jury with a recommendation to mercy because both men were under the influence of alcohol and the stabbing had occurred in the 'excitement' of the moment. The prosecution believed, however, that the first time Gough had left the beer house it was to collect the knife from his home which pointed to the act being premeditated. Justice Honeyman concurred with the guilty verdict and stated that he would put the jury's recommendation to the proper authorities but told Gough to hold out no hope for a reprieve from the death sentence.

II   Kicked to Death

The second murder trial was that of Charles Dawson who was charged with the murder of his paramour, Martha Jane Addison, at Darlington. Dawson was twenty-five and worked as a puddler. This was an occupation which required immense physical strength and stamina as it entailed the preparation of iron using a searing hot furnace. Dawson was also known to do a lot of poaching to top up his income. Originally from Barnard Castle, although she knew that he already had a wife who lived in Stockton, Martha had moved in with Dawson at Cleveland Street, Albert Hill in Darlington. She earned money by making and selling ginger beer to the workers at the nearby iron-works and contributed to the upkeep of the house. There were two rooms in Dawson's house and he and Martha occupied the room on the ground floor with three lodgers, Benny Harper, Patrick Dempsey and Thomas Mullens, occupying the room above.

At about 6 pm on Saturday 13 September 1873 Dawson, Martha and their three lodgers left the house to go for a drink in Northgate. Dempsey and Harper went off on their own and Mullens and the couple went into Brown's beer house where Dawson bought the drinks with Martha refusing to have anything. Dawson and Martha then left Mullens to visit a friend of theirs, Rachael Newton, where they had a glass of rum. For reasons unknown Dawson became aggressive towards Martha and slapped her on the head with the palm of his hand before leaving Rachael's house. Meanwhile, Mullens, Dempsey and Harper had joined up again in the King's Head and they later met Dawson who said that Martha had gone off. Mullens and Dawson returned to Rachael's looking for Martha but she was not there. By this time Dawson was becoming extremely agitated and said to Rachael 'when I light on her again I'll make it that she'll not run away so soon'. Rachael went to Cleveland Street to warn Martha that Dawson was in a foul mood but she received no reply to her knocking.

As Mullens and Dawson came to the railway crossing they met Martha who was heading towards home. Dawson approached her and dealt her a hard punch on the back which caused her to fall. Martha was crying and Dawson pulled her to her feet and led her home. She took the key from her pocket to unlock the door but Dawson grabbed it from her and, on opening the door himself, pushed Martha in telling her she had better pray because he was going to kill her. The two men then entered the house and Dawson locked the door behind them and put the key in his pocket. He then took off his coat and then lit a candle from the dying embers of the fire. As soon as the candle took hold he produced a revolver and pointed it at Mullens saying he would 'give him the contents of the weapon' if he raised any alarm. Dawson then picked up a bottle that was on the table and hit Martha over the head with it. She fell on her back and he threw the bottle at her but missed, the bottle smashing into pieces on the hard floor. Dawson began kicking the defenceless woman again and again with her letting out awful screeching noises. He then jumped on her throat and keeping one foot there began kicking her in the side with the other. After this Martha made no sound. Dawson's carried on with his attack by jumping up and down on her prone body. His feet never touched the floor until a knock was heard and Dempsey called out to open the door. Dawson stopped for a moment then jumped once more on Martha's throat before he calmly walked to the door, let Dempsey in, locked the door again and pocketed the key. Walking over to the fire he picked up the coal-rake and hit Martha with it four times. Dempsey shouted that the woman was dead but Dawson replied that she was not and lifting up a large earthenware basin full of dirty water he threw it over Martha shouting her name at the same time. Dawson told Dempsey to go and get some more water and unlocked the door for him. Dempsey got some water, left it at the door and then went to fetch a doctor. Mullen, taking advantage of the unlocked door, ran out and went for the police. By the time Dr Easby, Police Superintendent Richard Rogers and PC Stokoe arrived at the scene at about 11 pm the entire room was an utter shambles with broken glass, furniture overturned and blood-stains on the floor. Martha's head had been placed on a bolster pillow and her face had been washed but of Dawson there was no sign. The doctor pronounced Martha as deceased and her body was removed. The police made a search of the house and found firearms, these, along with the broken bottle, coal-rake and basin were removed as evidence. At about 2 am on Sunday morning Sergeant Cuthbert was on duty in Cleveland Street when he spotted Dawson's dog standing outside a house at the end of the road. On going to investigate he found Dawson inside and charged him with the murder of Martha to which there was no denial.

The post-mortem on Martha's body revealed a catalogue of injuries. There were multiple severe bruises on the face, head and body. The ears were full of blood and her earrings had been torn out, some of the teeth were knocked out and the upper lip was almost cut through. There was a large T-shaped wound on the back of the head and a thick mark across the throat. The cause of death was believed to be a blood clot to the brain probably caused by Dawson jumping on Martha's throat and cutting off her air and blood supply.

At the trial there was no doubt that Dawson had killed Martha, it only had to be decided whether it was manslaughter or murder. Had Dawson been so drunk that he was not in control of his actions? This was doubtful as it appeared, rather than sitting in a beer house drinking, he had spent most of the evening searching the town for Martha. After the jury had heard the results of the post-mortem and listened to the evidence of the two main witnesses, Mullens and Dempsey, there could have been little doubt in their minds that this was an unprovoked act of mindless violence. The verdict came back as guilty and once again during the Durham Winter Assizes a sentence of death was passed down.

III Slashed to Death

The third and final murder trial was that of William Thompson for the murder of his wife, Jane, at Annfield Plain on Saturday 4 October 1873. He had been apprehended at his brother's house in Dipton by Police Constable John Brown and charged with cutting his wife's throat.

Jane Johnson was born at Urpeth where her father, Edward, worked as miner. The family moved to Annfield Plain where Jane met and married Henry Atchison from Lanchester. The couple had a child and separated soon after with Jane going to live with relatives at Felling and it was there that she met twenty-five-year-old William Thompson. The couple were married at Gateshead Register Office in February 1872 despite strong objections from Jane's family as she and her first husband had not been divorced. Their wedded bliss did not last long and Jane left Thompson and went back to live with her father at Pontop Cottages, Annfield Plain. A few days later Thompson arrived and begged Jane to take him back as he would treat her 'more kindly' in the future. Jane decided to give him another chance and her father agreed to let him stay at his house. Everything seemed to be going well for the couple for about five weeks or so until a day trip to Newcastle heralded an unforeseen tragic sequence of events.

The village of Annfield Plain in the nineteenth century, home of William Thompson and his wife, Jane, until he slit her throat in 1873. Author's collection

Thompson was described as a short, dark complexioned man who did not have the appearance of someone who could take another's life. At the onset of the trial, with Mr Sowerby as counsel for the prosecution and Mr Skidmore for the defence, Thompson pleaded not guilty and gave his version of events which was that he and his wife had been arguing because they had gone into a public house in Newcastle to eat and she had gone off to talk to a man and left him sitting on his own 'like a child'. That night, after supper, the argument had flared up again and Thompson had struck Jane. She had then brandished a razor at him so he had chased her to the door of the house and struck her again. Jane had then turned the razor on herself cutting her own throat. Thompson agreed he was instrumental in her death but not responsible for the act.

The first witness to be called was Jane's father who stated that on the day in question his daughter and her husband had gone to Newcastle returning about 6.30 pm. The family sat and had their supper and Johnson then went to Dodd's Beer House to have a drink. As he left the house there did not appear to be anything amiss, Thompson was cutting up a rabbit with a large kitchen knife and Jane was sitting at the table watching him. A short time later a girl had come into the beer house saying that something had happened to Jane so her father had gone back to the house to see what was wrong. On hearing a commotion at his neighbour's house he entered to find his daughter lying on the floor with her clothes saturated with blood from

An old Auty postcard depicting Harelaw church at Annfield Plain. Author's collection

a fatal wound in her throat. Johnson also stated that he owned a black shafted razor that he had lent to his son-in-law but when he looked for it on Sunday morning it was nowhere to be found.

The next witness was Mary Ann Parker in whose house Jane had breathed her last. Her testimony was that on Saturday evening at about 8 pm she had heard a woman scream. A few seconds later Jane had rushed in, a gaping wound to her throat and her dress drenched in blood. She had fallen to the floor and Mary Jane held her until another neighbour, Anne Scullan, arrived. There were also three children and a pregnant woman in the house who had witnessed these events but it was decided that their evidence in court was not required. Mary Ann Hall and a young girl, Elizabeth Parker, were outside and had seen Thompson running away from the house.

By the time PC John Brown, PC Joshua Reay and Dr John Gilland Hunter attended the scene, Jane was dead. She had turned twenty in the previous July and left a child of about three without a mother. Johnson's house, where the couple had lived, was searched but no traces of violence or blood were found there. Dr Hunter later performed a post-mortem on the body and stated that death was due to the loss of blood from the wound to the throat. He thought it was quite feasible that Jane could have managed to get to the neighbour's house with such a wound as it would take a minute or so for the heart to pump the blood from her body. He added that he did not believe it was possible for Jane to have cut her own throat as it would have taken considerable force to inflict the long, deep wound. He believed that she was attacked from behind, her head pulled back and held still with the left hand while the right hand had used the weapon. He added that it was only the vertebrae of the spine that kept Jane's head attached to her body. In his opinion it was possible that if the perpetrator had carried out the act swiftly it was entirely possible that he would not have got any blood upon himself. The kitchen knife that Thompson had been using to cut up a rabbit shortly before Jane's death was produced as being a possible weapon but the doctor thought it was too jagged to have inflicted the wound and the instrument used was more likely to have been a straight-edged razor. It was believed that the razor belonging to Jane's father that could not be found had been the murder weapon.

Thompson's brother, Alexander, lived with his wife, Ann, at Dipton. At about 9 pm on the Saturday night Ann had come out of the pantry and was surprised to see her brother-in-law standing in the middle of the kitchen with a wild look on his face. Two neighbours, Barbara Kane and Sarah Nealley, came in just at that moment to

Lanchester village where William Thompson was committed to stand trial for the murder of his wife in 1873. Author's collection

see Thompson taking his shirt off and saying something about wanting a change of clothes. The three women were frightened by his appearance saying that he was acting like a lunatic. Ann had told him to leave and Thompson had sworn at them and said that 'he took the razor and slit her throat'. A local man, Thomas Palmer, accompanied PC Brown to show him where Thompson's brother lived. They arrived at the house just as Ann was telling her brother-in-law to leave. Thompson was arrested and taken to the police station at Consett. An initial inquest was held at the police court at Shotley Bridge and a second inquest at Lanchester where Thompson was committed to stand trial at Durham Assizes.

Palmer stated that as he and PC Brown had entered the house at Dipton Thompson had said 'Now, here's a man who knows me and knows what kind of a wife I have.' As he was being escorted out Thompson shouted goodnight to Ann and the others in the house saying that they would not see him again. Knowing that there had been no trace of blood found at the house where the couple had been last seen together Palmer asked the prisoner where he had last struck his wife. Thompson said it was outside the door and she had run one way and he the other.

Ann Grace Watson and Sarah Graham had been returning on Saturday from Newcastle on Mr Bone's brake (carriage) with Jane, her three-year-old daughter and William Thompson. They gave evidence as to what they had heard and observed on the journey. Thompson had been asking his wife about a man she had spoken to while they were in Newcastle. He asked what the man had said to her but Jane did not reply. On asking her a second time Jane had said 'get out with you' and turned her head away from her husband. Although Jane apparently did not think the matter worth discussing her husband had other ideas and, losing his temper swore at her and struck her. When the brake reached Pelton Bank Thompson had alighted for a few minutes. Before he returned Sarah asked Jane if he was her husband and she replied that he was and was jealous but there was no need as the man she had been talking to in Newcastle was her cousin. When the brake reached Oxhill Thompson asked Jane for money and when she refused Thompson hit her again and then threatened that when he got her home that it would be one or the other of them that night. Jane had begun to cry and said that he was right, it would be one or the other of them, but why did he only abuse her when her father was not around.

The defence brought two arguments on Thompson's behalf. Firstly, that his version of events may have been true and that Jane had taken her own life as there had been no blood on his shirt sleeves or his person when he was arrested but Dr Hunter's evidence had disputed this. Secondly, if the court believed that Thompson had been the perpetrator, then the verdict should be manslaughter as Jane had given him every reason to cause him to be jealous and to mistrust her. Both of these arguments were ignored and the jury returned a verdict of guilty of wilful murder against Thompson so death was the only sentence the law would allow.

The date of execution was set for Monday 5 January 1874, to be carried out by William Marwood who had taken over from Calcraft and Askern. Those whose duty it was to attend the execution must have felt relief because Marwood used the long drop which made it a lot less likely that the person on the end of the rope would be seen slowly strangling to death as on too many previous occasions. Financially an execution such as this, three for one, would mean only one lot of expenses for the executioner and a saving on joiners' fees as the gallows would only have to be erected once.

For the first time in the history of Durham executions the representatives of the press were forbidden to be present. The visiting justices of Durham gaol had passed a resolution to that effect. At 8 am the prison bell began to toll and continued to do so until 8.10 am when the black flag was hoisted as a sign that the sentence of the three murderers had been completed. No reason was ever forthcoming as

The Durham Cathedral clock would chime out a death knell to mark the hour as an execution took place. Author's collection

to why it took as long as ten minutes for the executions to be carried out but, although the authorities clearly did not want details of the manner of the deaths to be broadcast, there were still details revealed from the inquest on the bodies. Prison officials, medical men and a sworn jury were obliged to attend this morbid finale. It was from one of these sources that information was divulged. Gough and Dawson were said to have looked peaceful and calm in death but Thompson was said to 'have died hard'. Gough and Thompson had both turned to their religious advisers and admitted their guilt but Dawson had gone to his death with no confession or remorse on his lips.

CHAPTER 22

The Irish Miners
1874

n 1874 Dipton was an extensive colliery village housing a large number of Irish families whose men folk worked in the nearby pit. Near to the larger village was an area known as High Bush Blades which consisted of just four small houses. One of these was occupied by Phillip Burdy, his family and his brother Simon. A short distance away was another small area of housing known as Hill Top where Hugh Daley and his family lived.

Saturday drinking sessions among the men of the mining community were common. Long hours within the darkness and dust of the pit gave them good reason to want to wash out their throats and let off steam. On 7 November Daley, having received his wages, had been drinking all day. He arrived home so drunk that he was put to bed by his wife and a neighbour, Ann Smith, who was in the house at the time. A miner, John Power, was also present and witnessed the events that followed.

Dipton Colliery, situated between Consett and Stanley, where Phillip Burdy and Hugh Daley were employed as miners in 1874. Author's collection

To all accounts, in an innocent visit, Burdy arrived at the Daley's house shortly afterwards. For reasons that no one could explain, Daley jumped from his bed, picked up the poker from the fireside and hit Daley over the head with it. Power rushed out to tell Burdy's brother, Simon, what had happened. Burdy staggered into the nearest house where the occupant, Mrs Smith, dressed the wound. Burdy's cap had come off when the blow was struck and, rather foolishly, he went back to the Daley's to retrieve it. By this time word had spread about the attack and there were a few men hovering about. When Burdy entered Daley went for him again with the poker. Those present were too frightened to interfere in case they too were turned on.

Meanwhile, Simon, when informed of his brother's first injury, had gone to find PC Forester who was about a mile away from Hill Top. The constable ran as fast as he could to the scene and from a distance away heard the thumps which were the sound of the poker striking Burdy. When Daley saw the police uniform he threatened to kill him too and flew at Forester, wielding the poker in the air. As he brought it down Forester managed to jump out of the way and the weapon struck the ground taking the attacker off balance and causing him to fall. Before he could rise he was quickly overpowered and handcuffed.

The village of Lanchester where Hugh Daley was committed for trial for the murder of Phillip Burdy in 1874. Author's collection

Burdy was carried into Daley's house and a doctor sent for. The victim's face and head were barely recognisable as belonging to a human being having being turned almost to pulp by the attack. Dr Hunter, of Stebbhouse, arrived on the scene shortly after but there was nothing he could do and Burdy died about thirty minutes later.

The initial inquest was held at the Prince of Wales Inn at Flinthill where Dr Hunter gave his post-mortem report. He detailed multiple wounds, smashed bones and fractures of which any one could have been the fatal blow. Daley stated only that he did not want Burdy in his home, he had broken in and he had stopped him. A second inquest was held at Lanchester where Daley was committed to Durham Assizes for trial on the charge of wilful murder.

The case was heard before Baron Cleasby at the Winter Assizes where, with so many witnesses to the unprovoked attack, the trial was just a formality and the verdict could only be guilty. Daley was known as a drunken, idle, violent man who would not be missed, even by his wife. Burdy, on the other hand, had been well thought of by his co-workers. The two men had been on good terms prior to that fateful day so no one could understand the reason behind the brutal murder. Daley remained arrogant and uncooperative until he was executed by Marwood on Monday 28 December 1874.

CHAPTER 23

Murders and Executions
1875

I Poisonous Powder

A different judge presiding, different accused in the dock and different methods, but in a repeat of the previous year, the court at Durham had a busy schedule with four murder trials. The Autumn Assizes were heard before Justice Huddlestone who not only had to direct the jury on the fate of three men but also a woman. The first man tried was George Plummer for the murder of his fiancée, Sarah Forster. Plummer was found guilty but insane and was committed to a mental asylum for the rest of his life.

The second trial was that of Elizabeth Pearson who stood accused of murdering her uncle, James Watson, at his home in Gainford. Elizabeth was twenty-eight and married with a son. Her husband was John Pearson, an agricultural labourer, and although they had their own home Elizabeth had stayed at her uncle's house as housekeeper since the death of his wife. Watson was seventy-four and in poor health so perhaps Elizabeth thought she would hurry the process along hoping for an inheritance. As was common at the time there was also a lodger living in the house, a man named George Smith. Watson was being treated by Dr Homfrey who had prescribed pills for his illness. Elizabeth suggested that her uncle would find it easier to take powders mixed in liquid rather than trying to swallow pills and the doctor complied with this request. On Monday 15 March George Smith went to Elizabeth's mother-in-law, Jane Pearson, and told her that Watson had become extremely ill. Jane immediately went to the house and could see that the elderly man was indeed very ill and it also looked as though he was in terrible agony. Elizabeth was sitting by his bedside holding his wrists. Jane went to fetch some brandy but when she returned it was too late. In death Watson's head was thrown back, his teeth were clenched and his body taut as if he had died during a convulsion.

Dr Homfrey was a little concerned at the manner of death as Watson's illness had not been life threatening. Robert, Watson's son, was not convinced that his father's death had been a natural one. He had also noticed that since Elizabeth had lived with his father items from the house had been disappearing and Robert had already suspected Elizabeth of selling them. After speaking with Robert, Dr Homfrey decided to perform a post-mortem. He could find no apparent cause of death but thought that the organs looked dis-coloured and the contents of the stomach smelt suspicious so decided to send a portion of the liver and the stomach to the Leeds School of Medicine for analysis. The results showed large quantities of strychnine and iron cyanide in the stomach, the two main ingredients found in rat poison.

Immediately after her uncle's death Elizabeth had begun moving his furniture and smaller possessions to her own house, an act which cast further suspicion upon her and she was arrested. After an initial inquest it was decided there was enough evidence to commit her to the Assizes for murder.

The prosecution witnesses left no doubt that Elizabeth had murdered her uncle in a cold and calculated fashion with the motive being nothing more than greed. John Corner, a grocer, testified that Jane Pearson, on two separate occasions, had bought packets of Battles Vermin Killer from him saying that they were for her daughter-in-law because she had an infestation of mice at her house. Jane stated that Elizabeth had asked her not to say anything about the poison as her husband did not agree with mouse powders. The police had searched both Elizabeth's and her uncle's house and had found no trace of any powder being laid out and no trace of any mice. Robert Watson testified to the fact that articles had gone missing from his father's house since Elizabeth had taken on the role of housekeeper. Elizabeth denied any knowledge of mouse powder and stated that if that was what had killed her uncle then it must have been the lodger, George Smith, who had administered it.

The jury retired to deliberate and immediately dismissed the idea of Smith being involved as he had no motive at all. They returned a verdict of guilty of wilful murder against Elizabeth but with a recommendation for mercy. For the second time at Durham during the nineteenth century a sentence of death was passed on a woman for the poisoning of another human being. Elizabeth tried to avoid the ultimate punishment by saying she was pregnant but a police surgeon's examination showed this to be untrue.

II   No Motive

John Kilcran was a forty-two-year-old Irish labourer. Married with a wife and four children, he lived with his family in Church Street which ran from Park Street to the section of the River Skerne, opposite St Cuthbert's church in Darlington. The street was a smaller version of Albert Hill, mainly occupied by Irish families, some living in one room, and all in cramped squalor.

The twelfth century church of St Cuthbert in Darlington, situated near to where John Kilcran met his end in 1875. Michael Gilligan was hanged for murder and James Durkin and James Flynn received fifteen years in penal servitude for manslaughter. The author

At about 10 pm on Easter Sunday, 28 March 1875, Kilcran was walking along Park Street when he was accosted by a group of seven men. With no apparent provocation or motive one of the men pulled something from his pocket and struck Kilcran with it. Two more of the group commenced kicking the man in the head as he lay on the ground where he had fallen. A youth, John William Rickaby, who had witnessed the assault, went to inform the police. Mrs Kilcran called Dr James Howison to attend to her husband. The doctor found bruises above the eyes and also one large wound about three inches in length. Dr Howison considered this wound to be life threatening and told the police that the injured man might not survive.

James Durkin, James Flynn and Michael Gilligan were taken into custody on a charge of assault. The three men were brought up at Darlington police court on Wednesday, when Police Superintendent Richard Rogers of the Darlington police asked for a remand as it was not known whether the charge of assault was going to become a more serious one. After witnesses to the event had given their statements the prisoners were remanded in custody until the following Tuesday. By then, however, Kilcran had succumbed to his injury and passed away. PC John Bowman charged the three men separately with murder to which they all pleaded innocence saying they were not even at the scene when the attack took place. A second inquest was then held at Darlington with the result that the three men were committed to trial at the Assizes.

Mr Blackwell acted as defence for Gilligan, Mr Skidmore for Flynn and Durkin and Mr Luck and Mr Edge were prosecution for the Crown. Dr Howison and a surgeon, William Easby, both concurred in their findings that the head wound had been the cause of Kilcran's death. They thought that the weapon had been used with considerable violence and had been a hatchet, chisel or some similar iron tool. A portion of the skull was shown to the jury to demonstrate how the weapon had gone straight through the bone and into the brain.

Charles Oyston and the youth who had initially gone for the police, John Rickaby, both stated that on the night in question they had been talking together when they had seen seven men come from the direction of the Lord Nelson towards Park Street. Two of the men, whom they now knew as Durkin and Flynn, had walked over and made a point of looking directly into the witnesses faces and then returned to the group who were now standing still. Oyston and Rickaby saw Kilcran walk up the street towards the silent group. One man had walked up to Kilcran and punched him two or three times in the face. Then Gilligan had reached into his pocket and dealt

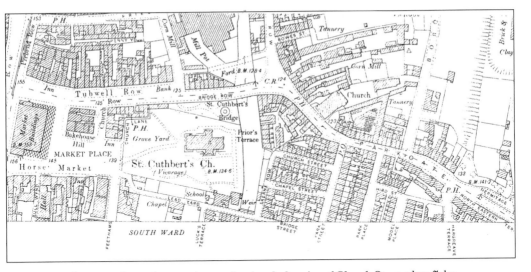

An extract from a large-scale map showing the location of Church Street where John Kilcran lived; and Park Street where he was murdered. Ordnance Survey, Darlington 1898

Kilcran a violent blow with whatever he had in his hand. Gilligan put the weapon back in his pocket and strolled off back towards the Lord Nelson. Two others of the group had kicked the defenceless man where he lay and then, all but one of the group, walked off leaving their victim lying bleeding in the street. Rickaby had gone for the police while Oyston and the seventh man from the group lifted Kilcran to take him to his house. A short way along they met Mrs Kilcran so she and Oyston carried her husband the rest of the way. Oyston stated that Durkin and Flynn were present but were not the men responsible for hitting or kicking the victim and Rickaby was not certain as to their identity, but both witnesses positively identified Gilligan as the man who had struck the fatal blow.

Ellen McCabe and Margaret and Sarah Burnside had been standing outside the Lord Nelson at about 10 pm on the night in question. They had seen Thomas Rooke, Felix Connofroy, Durkin and Flynn open the door and glance into the Malt Shovel and then into the Lord Nelson as if they were looking for someone. They had then, along with another three men, walked towards Park Street. The women had then heard someone groaning in pain and on going to investigate saw Kilcran on the ground. They had seen Durkin there but did not see him do anything and a few minutes later Oyston and another man had picked Kilcran up to carry him home. After all the evidence had been heard the prosecution suggested to the jury that Gilligan had dealt the murderous blow and that Durkin and Flynn had been accessories.

The jury came back with a verdict of guilty of wilful murder against Gilligan and guilty of manslaughter against Durkin and Flynn with a recommendation to mercy for all three because of their previous good characters. No motive, other than a fight between the Irish, was ever found and even though homes had been searched no weapon was ever discovered. All three men did not deny being in Park Street that night but still protested their innocence at any involvement in the crime. Gilligan stated that it had been an unfair trial and that the witnesses had sworn his life away. Kilcran had been known to have been in trouble with the law and was always fighting so they avoided him but had no grudge against him.

Justice Huddlestone addressed the court saying that he was satisfied that the jury had given a just verdict and he would pass the recommendation for mercy to the proper authorities. He told Gilligan that he had had a fairer trial than the one given to Kilcran so not to hold out hope of a reprieve as he had taken another man's life. Durkin and Flynn each received a sentence of fifteen years in penal servitude and Gilligan the death sentence.

III   The Drowned Man

On Sunday 11 April the body of a man was seen floating in the River Tees near the steps on the south side of Bridgegate, Barnard Castle. On the man being pulled from his watery grave the body was identified as being Thomas Mooney. His wife was currently serving a sentence in Northallerton gaol and their child had been living with Mooney's mother. Superintendent Thompson assisted to take Mooney's body to his mother's house where he searched his pockets. He found a small amount of silver, an empty purse and a newspaper. Mrs Mooney said that her son had collected some money for his employer that night which should have still been in his possession. Thompson then went back to where the body had been pulled from the water and was handed a handkerchief that had been found on the wall nearby. This was thought to belong to Mooney as he usually wore one tied around his neck. Initially it was thought that Mooney had fallen into the river, perhaps drunk, and drowned. A post-mortem was carried out by Dr John Mitchell who found that the cause of death was indeed drowning but there were injuries found that, in his opinion, were sustained prior to death. There were four wounds to the face, two of which were inflicted before death, and two of which

The River Tees at Bridgegate, Barnard Castle where Thomas Mooney was drowned in 1875. The author

he could not be absolutely certain. None of the wounds would have been fatal. There were no signs that Mooney had struggled after coming into contact with the water which pointed to him being unconscious before he drowned.

A nineteenth century view of Bridgegate, Barnard Castle. Author's collection

The police began to make enquiries as to Mooney's movements before his death. As a result of their findings William McHugh, William Gallagher, Thomas Brannen and Edward (Teddy) Keenan were taken into custody on suspicion of having some involvement in the drowning. At the initial inquests Brannen and Keenan were cleared of any wrongdoing but McHugh and Gallagher were charged with murder and committed to trial at the Assizes.

With Mr Blackwell defending and Mr Skidmore prosecuting Brannen and Keenan gave their version of events as the two principal witnesses at the trial. After the public houses had closed on Saturday night they had gone to Gallagher's house to carry on drinking. Mooney and McHugh had followed them in shortly after. Keenan and Mooney had begun to argue and Keenan had given him a push but before it came to blows Brannen pulled Keenan away and they left. Brannen's handkerchief was left behind, which turned out to be the one found near the river. Brannen lived at Mortham, about three miles from Barnard Castle, and as it was too late for him to get home, by this time it was the early hours of Sunday morning, they knocked on the door of a lodging house but could get no answer. They decided to go to Pat Finns', a friend of theirs and as they were walking they saw McHugh and Gallagher holding a man between them and going towards the river. They propped the man on the wall and the witnesses, who had followed but thought they had not been seen, heard McHugh say 'Is that the water? Throw him in'. Gallagher answered that he would not so McHugh pushed the man, whom by now the witnesses recognised as Mooney, into the water. Gallagher had no shoes on and as he headed back to his house he fell twice. Brannen and Keenan skirted round them and arrived at the passage-way beside Gallagher's house just ahead of McHugh who, when he saw them, held his hand up and said 'Not a word about this.' The two witnesses then went to Finns' house and sat upon his step until he opened his door at 5 am. They had breakfast there and afterwards Brannen went back to Mortham and Keenan went to Gallagher's house at about 9 am. Gallagher was shouting about someone breaking his pipe and began threatening him so in fear for his life, even forgetting to pick up his hat, he went back to Finn's.

The landlord of Dobson's Beer House, Thomas Dobson, said after the body was found Gallagher and McHugh were on his premises and he could not help but hear most of their conversation. They had been talking about a handkerchief and then Gallagher had said 'Confess and hang Teddy. If thou doesn't hang Teddy thou'll be transported for life.' Dobson left the room for a few moments and

The Butter Market in Barnard Castle in 2005. This octagonal building was once used as the town lock-up as well as for selling dairy produce. The author

when he returned heard McHugh say 'Thou does not mean to say I did it.' Gallagher answered 'Yes, thou did the deed and I'm speaking the truth the same time as I'm saying it.' Anthony Chapman had also been in the beer house that night and heard most of the same conversation. George Welford had said to Gallagher that if a man was drunk he might fall down the steps into the river. Gallagher had replied 'Mooney did not go down the steps, he went over the wall. The man was dead when he went over the wall.' Welford then accused Gallagher of knowing something about what had happened and the answer to this was 'Oh I do, do I?'

Although there was no physical evidence to connect McHugh to the crime the witness statements were overwhelming and the jury brought in a verdict of guilty against thirty-five-year-old McHugh but Gallagher was cleared. McHugh was shouting his innocence as Justice Huddlestone passed down sentence of death.

On Saturday 31 July a note was received from the Home Office with regard to the fate of the three condemned prisoners which read as follows:

Sir, In reply to your letter of the 10th instant I am directed by Mr Secretary Cross to acquaint you that he does not propose advising any interference with the course of the law in the case of Michael Gilligan,

Elizabeth Pearson and William McHugh now under sentence of death for wilful murder.

I am yours obediently, AFO Liddell

On Monday 2 August 1875, the day set for the executions, no members of the press were admitted to watch events from within the gaol so had to be satisfied with standing outside the gates amongst the crowd of curious spectators that had assembled. Two men who introduced themselves as being reporters from Barcelona in Spain, had travelled from Newcastle hoping to witness an English execution to see if it differed from those in their country. They were to be disappointed as they were also refused admission to the grounds. At 7.45 am the death bell began to toll and soon after the three prisoners were led to the scaffold, pinioned and hooded. Elizabeth Pearson was the first be hanged and the two men, Michael Gilligan and William McHugh immediately afterwards. By 8.03 am the black flag was hoisted and it was all over. The executioner, Marwood, as was customary, waited for the inquest on the bodies and left Durham immediately afterwards. Those that attended the inquest reported that the bodies, in their coffins with only their heads and clasped hands showing, looked calm enough to be asleep. Except for the whiteness of their skin and a deep, dark ring around McHugh's neck, one would not have known that these three had met their end by the rope.

All three were buried in unmarked graves within the grounds of the gaol. Elizabeth Pearson was buried next to her fellow poisoner, Mary Ann Cotton, the only other woman to have been executed at Durham in the nineteenth century.

Chapter 24

He Shot His Brother-in-Law 1876

I t was quite common for large families and relations to live together in mining villages and share any money that was earned. The house where this tragedy took place was no exception. Elizabeth Green, a widow, her two sons by a previous marriage, John and Joseph Wales and her daughter lived in a small property in Edmondsley. Elizabeth's daughter was married to John Williams who, along with their five children also lived in the same house. Both the Wales brothers, Williams and three of his sons all worked as miners at Byron Pit. On Friday 23 June 1876 Williams had returned from work, washed himself and gone to bed. One of his sons followed soon after with £6, the fortnight's wages for their father, his two brothers and himself. He handed the money to his mother who sorted out her bills and placed the rest on table at the end of the bed. When Williams got up at about 6.30 pm he asked his wife for some money. She told him where it was lying and he lifted a sovereign and went out. When his wife noticed that he had taken a sovereign and Williams had not returned after an hour or so Mary, his youngest daughter, was sent to tell him to come home and return the money but he had still not returned at 9 pm. His wife was worried because he had been drinking very heavily lately and even more since the death of his mother a short while previously. It was not just the fact that they could not afford to spend money on drink it was also because Williams had become nasty and aggressive with her when under the influence of alcohol. She decided to go herself and try to get him to come home. When she found him at the Black Horse a heated argument took place so his wife decided it would be prudent to hide in the back room of the public house.

At about 10 pm Williams returned home drunk and in a foul mood. He loaded a gun and young Mary asked him what he was going to do with it. His answer was that he was going to shoot her mother. Williams went to the Black Horse but when the landlord, James Hardy, would not let him in he returned home. Elizabeth tried to talk him into putting the gun down but he ignored her and, becoming

The village of Sacriston, from where Sergeant Smith came to arrest John Williams in 1876. Author's collection

extremely worried, she went out to alert the police. As Elizabeth left the house she met her daughter and her two sons, John and Joseph, coming towards the house and told them what had occurred. Her daughter ran to get the police and she and her sons went back to the house but the door was bolted from the inside so they forced it open and went in. Elizabeth saw Williams rise from the chair he had been sitting in, point the gun and shoot. Her son, John, fell to the floor and she could see that his right arm was on fire. Elizabeth managed to extinguish the flames with her hand and then saw blood running down Wales's arm. As she went to leave the house to call for help her daughter ran in and grabbed the gun from her husband's hand and threw it in the rain tub. Sergeant Smith of Sacriston arrived and arrested Williams charging him with attempted murder. A doctor attended the wounded man, who, although in great pain, was conscious.

The initial inquest was heard at Durham County Police Court on Saturday where all the witnesses were called to give evidence. A doctor had handed in a certificate to the court in regards to the critical condition of the injured man. Williams was remanded in custody. Wales died on Sunday night as a direct cause of his wound so the charge was now murder.

Williams stood trial at Durham Assizes before Justice Lush on Wednesday 5 July with Mr Greenhow as counsel for the defence and Mr Granger and Mr Edge for the prosecution. All the witnesses were called to give their evidence a second time. The medical evidence as to the cause of the victim's death was that he had suffered a compound fracture of the arm, shoulder and collar bone, a severed artery and the ramrod had punctured his lung. Mr Greenhow put forward in William's defence that there was no motive for him to murder his brother-in-law and that he was drunk and the gun went off by accident so the charge should be reduced to manslaughter. If Williams had just loaded the gun with powder it would have done no damage but he had left the ramrod in the barrel and it was this that had been fired at close range and caused the wound. All the witness testimony, however, proved that Williams had been threatening to shoot his wife and had shot Wales instead. Justice Lush summed up by saying that the jury had three options. If they believed that the gun had gone off by accident then Williams must be found not guilty and acquitted. If they believed that he had not known the ramrod was still in the gun but had deliberately fired at Wales then

he was guilty of manslaughter. If they believed that he did know the ramrod was still in the gun and had deliberately fired at Wales then he was guilty of wilful murder. After retiring for twenty minutes the jury returned a verdict of guilty of wilful murder, the black cap was donned and sentence of death passed. The sentence was carried out on Wednesday 26 July 1876 by William Marwood.

The executioner, William Marwood, who hanged John Williams for shooting and killing his brother-in-law, John Wales, in 1876.
Author's collection

CHAPTER 25

Evil or Insane?
1878

Robert Vest, from Seaham, was married with five children. He had been unemployed for some time until, in June 1878, he obtained work as a ship's steward, which involved doing all the meals aboard the barque, *William Leckie*. The vessel was moored at Sunderland Roads waiting for a favourable wind and tide to set sail with a crew of twenty and a cargo of coal for Montevideo in South America. The captain was Lumley Fletcher and the sixty-two year-old pilot was John Wallace. Both were well known and respected seamen. On the morning of Wednesday 26 June Captain Fletcher had left on a train for Newcastle to obtain the necessary papers for his vessel to leave port. At about 4 pm when he returned to the ship, which was lying at anchor about two miles offshore, the crew were

The Port of Sunderland where the William Leckie *was moored when Robert Vest stabbed John Wallace to death in 1878.* Author's collection

amusing themselves with different pastimes to while away the time. Coming across Vest he noticed that he appeared to be drunk when he should have been preparing a meal for the crew. Fletcher immediately checked on the ship's liquor stores but none of the seals were broken so he assumed Vest must have brought alcohol aboard himself which was strictly forbidden. The captain and his pilot, Wallace, confronted Vest and told him they would not tolerate drunkenness on board and threatened that he could be reduced to the rank of a common seaman because of his actions. Vest was then told he was relieved of his duties for the rest of that day until he could pull himself together. Fletcher then ordered a cask of rum to be opened and all the crew were given a glass. All, that is, but Vest, Fletcher said he had had enough to drink already. Vest scuttled off and must have harboured thoughts of revenge over the discipline he had received.

A short while later Thomas Talbot, an apprentice, Richard Smith and John Moss, two members of the crew, the boatswain and the carpenter were all on deck when they heard Wallace shout that he had been stabbed. They all ran to the water closet, where the shout had come from, to see Vest in the closet with the pilot brandishing a large Bowie knife. As the crew approached Vest, holding Wallace by the collar in his left hand, struck him a violent blow in the stomach with the knife in his right hand. Wallace staggered from the closet pulling the knife from his stomach as he did so and then fell onto the deck. Because Wallace had been using the water closet his trousers were not fastened so the gaping wound where the knife had gone in up to its hilt was in full view. The pilot's bowels were protruding and he also had a large, deep gash to his throat. By this time the rest of the crew and Fletcher had arrived. Brandy and bandages were sent for but Wallace was dead before they could be brought. Vest gave no resistance as some of the crew took hold of him and, on the Captain's instructions, lashed him to the deck. Word was sent ashore and Sergeant James Larkin and three police officers proceeded to the vessel on the tug *Champion*. They took the prisoner into custody and conveyed him to the Low Street Police Station.

At the initial inquest Vest accused Fletcher of threatening to punish him as no man had been punished before, to put him ashore without a stitch of clothing and that he had been run round the deck by Walker. Fletcher denied all the allegations saying that he had only threatened to demote Vest to a seaman because he thought he was drunk. Although never proven one way or the other it is doubtful that Vest had been drinking as no-one had seen him with alcohol, and the seals on the rum kegs had not been tampered with. It was felt by all that had been aboard the vessel that Fletcher had been Vest's initial target but he had come across Wallace first and taken his rage out on him instead. Vest was found guilty at the inquest and committed to stand trial at the following Durham Assizes.

On Friday 12 July Vest stood trial before Justice Baggally accused of wilful murder. Since the event Vest had tended to ramble and did not appear to be entirely sane. It came to light that he had joined the army when he was seventeen and had been sent to India where he had suffered sunstroke. He had also served in the Crimean War where he had sustained head injuries. Vest's family said that prior to this he had been a normal young man but had changed after all his sufferings. A letter had been procured from the War Office confirming that Vest had received head injuries caused by an exploding shell. The day of the murder had been the hottest that could be remembered for many years. It would have been stifling below deck on board the vessel so Vest and the other crew were on the top deck in the blazing heat. It was suggested by the defence that this could have had a bearing on Vest's actions. Dr Matthew Francis gave evidence that it was quite possible that Vest did suffer a form of insanity and the heat could have caused him to lose control of normality.

The prosecution pointed out that Vest had been violent on more than one occasion previously. He had been incarcerated in Durham gaol for an attack on a gas manager at Seaham, and shortly after he was released he had threatened violence towards a seaman. It was argued that it was because he was drunk and looking for revenge on the authority which had reprimanded him that he had wilfully taken an old man's life.

The jury found Vest guilty but with a very strong recommendation to mercy. Justice Baggally gave his closing statement saying, that because the verdict was guilty, he must pass the only sentence the law would allow which was death. The recommendation for mercy would be passed to the proper authorities and the prisoner would have to await the outcome. A petition was signed by numerous people of the area and forwarded to the Home Secretary but to no avail, a reprieve was not granted and Robert Vest was hanged by William Marwood on Tuesday 30 July 1878.

There were many recorded cases of extremely harsh treatment aboard ship and no one but Vest, Fletcher and Wallace could have known exactly what was said or threatened during the altercation regarding Vest's condition on that day. Perhaps Vest was mentally disturbed, the events certainly point in that direction, and whatever he was threatened with pushed him over the edge. Of the three men involved in the tragedy only one survived and the whole sorry affair gives rise to the question on whether his conscience would have been clear or whether he would have been haunted by the fact that his words ultimately caused the death of two men.

CHAPTER 26

The Shoemaker and the Farm Girl 1880

On Wednesday 18 August 1880 William Teesdale was walking home across fields between Evenwood and Cockfield when he saw a man and a woman lying face down on the ground near the footpath. On going to investigate he could see immediately that the woman was dead. Her clothes were saturated with blood that had come from a large deep gash to her throat. The man, who also had a wound to his throat, was alive but, although his eyes were open, he did not answer when spoken to. Teesdale ran back the way he had come to where some people were working in a turnip field and the farmer and labourers took a cart and conveyed the couple

The church of St Mary the Virgin at Cockfield in 2006. It was in a field between this village and Evenwood where William Brownless lay in wait for Elizabeth Holmes with murder as his intent. The author

to Evenwood. The man was twenty-two-year-old William Brownless, who worked as a shoemaker at Butterknowle; the dead woman was twenty-five-year-old Elizabeth Holmes of Bishop Auckland.

Brownless was a powerfully-built man who was thought of in the area as a worthless good-for-nothing having served three months in gaol for breaking into Mrs Joplin's grocery shop at Evenwood. He drank heavily and, when under the influence of alcohol, became nasty and violent. Elizabeth, a short, stout woman, came from a well respected family who had kept public houses in Bishop Auckland. At the time of her death she had been living with her twin sister and her husband and working in the fields of Ralph Vart's farm. Elizabeth met Brownless through James Mills, her sister's husband, and the two became sweethearts. On the night before the tragedy the couple had gone for a walk and when she returned Elizabeth told her sister that she would not be seeing Brownless again. She gave no reason for this but appeared adamant in her decision. The following morning Elizabeth left the house to go to work as usual carrying her hoe and a satchel containing her dinner and was not seen alive again.

Sergeant Banks and Police Constable Thorn of Bishop Auckland were called to investigate the crime. Around quite a wide area from where the couple had been found the grass was trampled and blood-soaked. Elizabeth's hoe, satchel, shawl and hat were found scattered about showing that there had been a considerable struggle. The victim had a minor and a severe gash to her throat giving rise to the

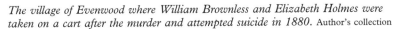

The village of Evenwood where William Brownless and Elizabeth Holmes were taken on a cart after the murder and attempted suicide in 1880. Author's collection

The church of St Paul at Evenwood in 2006. The author

impression that there had been more than one attempt to finish her off. Brownless, who had been taken to the Drover's Inn, also had two wounds as if the knife had been drawn forward and back again. He had lost a lot of blood but his wound was stitched and he survived.

Whether out of sympathy for the injured man or in a bid to procure a confession, Brownless was told that Elizabeth was still alive. He admitted that, knowing the route she took to work, he had been hiding by the hedge waiting for her. As she passed he had grabbed her legs and pulled her to the ground and drawn a razor across her throat. Elizabeth had managed to get up and run a few yards but Brownless caught up to her and cut her throat again. When he thought she was dead he drew the razor across his own throat and put the weapon in his breast pocket, then could remember no more until he recovered in the inn. Although he and the area of the crime were searched, no weapon was ever found.

No reason was ever forthcoming as to why Elizabeth had ended the relationship with her sweetheart but she paid the ultimate price for doing so. Brownless was also to pay the ultimate price when he was found guilty of her murder at the August Durham Assizes and Justice Field pronounced sentence of death.

There was snow on the ground and a freezing chill in the air on Tuesday 16 November 1880 as Brownless was led, pinioned, to the

Cottages at Evenwood in 2006. The author

scaffold. He was hanged by William Marwood. When the rope was placed around the victim's neck a small trickle of blood seeped down his shirt from the wound on his throat but within seconds the lever was pulled and his sorry life was over.

CHAPTER 27

He Wanted to Hang
1882

On Saturday 20 February 1869 Maria Fitzsimmons was found stabbed to death under the bed in her dirty, sparsely furnished room in a house in Baine's Lane, Sunderland. Maria, who was about forty at the time, had suffered twelve stab wounds to the back and heart which had been inflicted in what appeared to be a frenzied attack. There was a large amount of the blood on the bed and floor. On investigation it was thought that, initially, she was stabbed in the chest whilst lying on the bed and, as she tried to turn to get away, she received the wounds to her back. She then had, perhaps, landed on the floor and been stabbed again and crawled under the bed to die. Maria was known as an 'unfortunate', a prostitute and a woman who would get money wherever and however she could and then usually spent every penny on alcohol. Sunderland port provided rich pickings for women such as her as many of the men who had been at sea for months would step onto dry land craving for nothing more than to spend their hard-earned money on drink and the company of women. Whatever Maria's way of life, she did not deserve to die prematurely and in such a brutal fashion. She was entitled to justice but it was to be many years before justice was served. A reward of £100 was offered for information leading to the arrest and conviction of the perpetrator but to no avail.

An inquest was held at the Butcher's Arms in Coronation Street where a friend of Maria's, Dorothy Wilkinson, gave evidence. They had lived opposite each other and on the Saturday afternoon Maria, followed by a man, had called in to see her. The man was a stranger to Dorothy but she guessed he was a sailor by his manner of dress. Maria was 'stupid drunk' and the man kept telling her to return his coat and stockings or he would 'take the money back.' The couple had then gone over the road to Maria's lodgings, kissing and holding hands on the way. Although other neighbours had seen Maria with the man none had recognised him as anyone they knew but all agreed that he was a sailor. His appearance was described as 'dirty and unwashed' and his clothes consisted of a blue guernsey with a hole in the shoulder, a pair of fustian trousers and a cheese-cloth cap. His hair was a ginger colour and he spoke with either an Irish or an American accent.

On 20 March a pocket book and newspaper cuttings relating to the murder were found in the Serpentine River in London and these were passed to the Sunderland police. This gave rise to the idea that the perpetrator may have managed to leave the area aboard a sailing vessel. Then, on 27 March, a man's body was found in Hartlepool harbour. The body had been in the water for some time so the features were unrecognisable but, by the height and clothing, it was thought that this may have been the murderer; however, the police eventually ruled that possibility out. In April 1869 a man, again fitting the description of the murderer, wearing a blue guernsey with a hole in the shoulder, was arrested in Wapping. Peter Conner denied the charge and stated he had never been out of Gravesend in his life and had certainly never set foot in Sunderland. He added that he had been working at Messrs Whellock and Sons for the last twelve years and that his employers would verify that fact. James Gilhooley, one of the witnesses, was asked to travel to Wapping to identify the prisoner but he told the police that Conner was not the man he had seen with Maria on that fateful day. Conner lost a week's wages because of being wrongfully kept in custody. There was no other information forthcoming and the case was marked as unsolved.

Thirteen years later the prison director at Pentonville contacted the authorities to tell them that one of the prisoners had made a verbal and then a written confession on a slate to the murder of a woman at Sunderland in 1869. The wheels were put in motion very quickly and in April 1882 Thomas Fury, alias Charles Henry Cort, alias Thomas Wright, stood trial before Justice Williams at Durham Assizes. Fury had begun a fifteen year sentence in August 1879 and was taken to Pentonville in October 1881. He was an intelligent man who had turned his talents to crime and alcohol and he did not function well in confined areas or take kindly to authority. He had been taken to task three or four times for misdemeanours since he had been incarcerated and the punishment would have been extremely harsh. It appears that Fury felt that spending another fourteen years in the situation he found himself would be intolerable and losing his life was the preferable option.

His plea was 'guilty' and Justice Williams pointed out to him that his word alone was not enough and that it was the law of the land that this had to be proven by corroborating evidence and that he was entitled to defence. Fury, accordingly, changed his plea to not guilty

An early view of Pentonville Gaol where Thomas Fury was incarcerated in 1882 when he confessed having murdered Maria Fitzsimmons in 1869. Author's collection

and Mr Milvain consented to defend him against Mr Skidmore for the prosecution. As witnesses were called the links in the chain of circumstantial evidence were put together to form a whole. The first witness was William Lawrence who, in 1869, had been a seaman on board the *Lollard,* a schooner moored at the Pantiles at Sunderland. One of the crew was a man named Thomas Wright with whom Lawrence went ashore on Friday 19 February and, on walking up the main street, Wright went into a shop and bought two knives, one of which he gave to Lawrence. They then went to the Wear Music Hall and later for a drink at a public house near Baines Lane. Lawrence then went back aboard the schooner and he next saw Wright at about 7 pm on Saturday. Wright smelled strongly of drink, his face was scratched and he had a cut finger. He told Lawrence that he had been drugged and lost his money. Later that night someone related to the murder investigation had come aboard and looked at all the ship's crew's faces with a bull's eye lantern. Although the police suspected that the murderer was a sailor the *Lollard* was allowed to leave port a few days later. The vessel sailed for London and there Wright jumped ship taking with him some clothes and a pocket book belonging to Lawrence which was identified as the one found in the Serpentine River in March of 1869. Albert Snaith, who had been master of the *Lollard* in 1869, was called and confirmed the evidence that Lawrence had given relating to Wright jumping ship at London. He told the court that he thought the prisoner was the man he had known as Thomas Wright but he could not be sure. All the neighbours who had seen Maria's male companion on the day she died gave their statements and all thought that the prisoner resembled the man but none could be absolutely certain.

Fury's confession included all the facts related in the court, including the name he had used aboard ship and the fact that he had cut the tendons in his finger. He stated that he and Maria were drunk and she had stolen 15s (75p) from him so he had attacked her in a drunken rage.

The defence addressed the jury saying that Fury may be willing to commit suicide to save him from penal servitude and there was nothing in the confession that an intelligent man could not have discovered by other means than committing the crime. If the jury felt that he was guilty then it should only be manslaughter as there was no proof that it was murder. The prosecution argued that Fury's knowledge of events was too detailed for him not to have gone through the events personally and that this had been a cold-blooded murder. The jury were out just over an hour before returning a verdict of guilty. Fury had written letters while he had been incarcerated in Durham gaol and some of these were handed to the press after his death. He had intended writing about his life but felt, should it be published, others might follow the evil road he had taken. He had no wish to live and, as to dying early, he wrote that he was 'old' and it was not age but what he had done that had made him old.

Thomas Fury's death wish was granted when he was hanged by William Marwood on Tuesday 16 May 1882. He was the first executed criminal at Durham to have a white hood placed over his head and face so, whatever his countenance at the time of death, it was not visible to the public. His body was buried within the grounds of the gaol and covered with quicklime and, at last, justice had been served.

CHAPTER 28

A Gruesome Execution
1883

n January of 1883, at Sunderland Register Office, eighteen-year-old Elizabeth Ann Sharpe married James Burton, a ship's fireman. She was advised against marrying thirty-three-year-old Burton because of the vast difference in ages. There was also talk that he was already married and had a wife and family still living. Sadly, Elizabeth was love-struck and did not heed the advice. The couple were only weeks into their marriage when Elizabeth decided for some unrecorded reason that she did not like married life after all. She left her husband and went to work as a domestic for a solicitor, Mr Brewis, in Sunderland. On Tuesday 8 May at about 8.30 pm an engine driver, John Stevenson, saw an umbrella on the railway line at Tunstall. As he went to pick it up he saw a young woman lying in a ditch beside the tracks. He went to take a closer look and realised that the woman was dead. The body was lying face down with eight large pieces of limestone on top of it, three of which were on the head. Stevenson moved some of the limestone and could then see that the woman's head had been battered in. He went for help and the body was identified as being Elizabeth Burton. Because it was common knowledge that the couple had had problems a search was immediately launched to find her husband. Burton was apprehended the following day in Sunderland and there was no doubt in anyone's mind that he was the murderer as his clothes were saturated with blood. In his pocket were found two empty laudanum bottles.

The initial inquest was heard at the Half Moon Inn in Sunderland where numerous witnesses made statements. It was established that Burton had been begging Elizabeth to return to him and at about 7 pm on Tuesday evening he had called for her and they had gone out together. A little later Elizabeth had been seen running up the embankment with her husband chasing her. A scream had then been heard coming from the direction of the bridge over which the Ryhope and Silksworth railway passed. After all the evidence had been heard Burton was committed for trial. He stood before Justice Hawkins at

Durham Assizes where he was found guilty of murder and sentenced to death.

William Marwood was the executioner employed to hang Burton at 8 am on Monday 6 August 1883. Marwood had arrived in Durham on the Saturday afternoon and booked into the Dun Cow Inn which was situated just opposite the gaol. Everything for the execution had been put in readiness on Saturday evening, even the pole which would display the black flag was in place, so it was expected that the event would go smoothly and quickly. It was not to be. As was the usual practice, Marwood pinioned the prisoner in his cell but, as the strap above his elbow was being fastened, Burton had complained three times that it was too tight but his concerns were ignored. He was led to the scaffold with Marwood behind him, keeping his hand on the pinioning straps at a spot between the elbows. Following were the gaol officials, the chaplain, the surgeon and three members of the press. A rope had been placed to mark where the entourage should stop, which was almost underneath the instrument of death, so that they had a very limited view of the trap doors. The two main players climbed the stairs and Marwood grasped the pinioning straps to force Burton to a position under the beam. He then forced the man to move again so that he was facing west. The noose was placed around his neck and the lever pulled but those watching gave a cry of horror as the slack of the rope caught under Burton's arm. Instead of the noose tightening it caught under his chin and the hapless man went through the trap doors swinging by his shoulder and elbow. Although the spectators did not have a clear view, it was reported that the white hood had slid up. There was blood oozing where the rough rope had caught his skin and his face was contorted in agony. Marwood acted with lightening speed pulling the rope to the edge of the pit where two warders assisted him to lift the man out. The warders held the wretched man while Marwood released the rope from where it was caught under his elbow, readjusted the noose and violently hurled Burton into the pit. Once again the rope was seen to swing about wildly and it was obvious that the man on the end had an extremely painful death

The surgeon recorded death by strangulation as Burton's neck was swollen and elongated and his face contorted but, as no one but Marwood had a view of the pit, it was not known whether Burton had suffered for only seconds or minutes. There were suggestions that Marwood was drunk as accommodation was always given within the gaol but he had insisted on staying at an inn and it was known that he often had a drink whilst entertaining listeners with his exploits.

The Dun Cow Inn opposite the gaol at Old Elvet in Durham. It was here that the executioner William Marwood stayed in 1883 on the night before he hanged James Burton. The author

The sign that hangs above the door on the Dun Cow Inn. The author

Marwood denied the accusation and stated that Burton had gone into a faint and as he fell back and the trap doors opened his arm had caught in the slack of the rope. At the inquest on the body the coroner asked two questions:

Question 1: *Was he lifted out by the arm or the rope?*
Reply: *The rope.*
Question 2: *Do you consider the hangman was sober?*
Reply: *Yes, I think so.*

The reason behind this bungled execution could have been down to the state of Marwood's health at that time as he died in September of that same year of inflammation of the lungs and jaundice.

After Burton's death a confession giving the circumstances leading up to the murder in the form of a letter to Elizabeth's parents came to light. He had written that, while he and Elizabeth were walking she had dropped a note and when Burton had picked it up to hand it back to her she had poked him with her umbrella. Elizabeth had then started shouting at him that she would have her father and brother take care of him. Burton had reached for her, although not in a threatening manner, and she had attacked him with the umbrella again. His temper then got the better of him and he had struck her. Elizabeth had begged him not to hit her again and said she would return home with him but Burton wrote that his anger and passion blinded him and he picked up a stone and hit her with it. Elizabeth had fallen where she had been found and Burton, seeing immediately that she was dead, threw some limestone rocks on top of her and ran off to Sunderland. He had then bought some laudanum intending to kill himself but the attempt at suicide was unsuccessful. He wrote that he was truly sorry and wanted to be laid to rest beside Elizabeth as she was his wife and his best friend. His last wish was ignored and he was buried, as the law dictated, in an unmarked grave within the walls of the prison.

CHAPTER 29

Revenge on a Blackleg
1883

On the evening of Saturday 1 April 1882 Thomas Pyle, a plate-layer from Ushaw Moor, had gone drinking in Durham. He was in such a state of intoxication that he was helped by two young men to walk up Prior's Path. Pyle then lay down at the hedge side and fell asleep. He was seen by quite a few people, as they made their way home, still lying in the same spot at midnight. The following morning Pyle's dead body was discovered at a distance of some thirty yards from where he had been seen sleeping.

A post-mortem of the body being carried out at the Durham Infirmary by Dr Jepson and Dr Oliver established that Pyle had been murdered. His left arm was fractured, there was a hole in his wind-pipe and his throat had been crushed almost to a pulp – by a

A view of Ushaw Moor Colliery in the nineteenth century, where Thomas Pyle was employed as a platelayer before his murder by Peter Bray in 1882. Author's collection

Durham Infirmary where the post-mortem on Thomas Pyle's body was performed in 1860. Author's collection

beating. Although the police conducted many interviews and pieced together the dead man's last movements it was to be more than twelve months before there was an arrest, even though a reward of £200 was offered for information leading to the arrest and conviction of Pyle's murderer.

Peter McDonnell was born in Halifax in 1851 and he and his sister, Mary, when both young, were brought to Durham with their parents. After their father's death their mother married John Bray and the two McDonnell children adopted his surname. Young Peter Bray was always in trouble and was a general nuisance to his neighbours. He was sent to work in a carpet factory but decided he wanted employment in the pits. In 1866, at the age of fifteen, Bray began his criminal career, an assault for which he was imprisoned for seven days. Then in March 1873 he began a sentence of six months for cutting and wounding.

In 1874 Crossgate Peth (Path) leading from the city of Durham to Brandon and other pit villages, became a black spot for robberies on dark nights, often carried out with brutal violence. Eventually the police managed to arrest five of the perpetrators who were given long sentences of penal servitude and suffered the lash for their crimes. Two others, James Glancey and Bray, managed to escape. Glancey was arrested soon after for another crime and received a life

Castle Garth in Newcastle, where Peter Bray was eventually arrested for the murder of Thomas Pyle. Author's collection

sentence. With the assistance of the police at Newcastle, Bray was eventually arrested at the Castle Garth in 1875. He was sentenced to be incarcerated for seven years – and to be flogged. Bray was released in the early part of 1881 and went to live at Bearpark and enlisted in the Durham Militia. While undergoing his army training at Hartlepool he received a sentence of seven days, to be spent in Durham gaol, for drunkenness. As Bray left the prison on completion of his sentence, on 6 July 1883, the police were already waiting and arrested him on suspicion of the murder of Thomas Pyle.

Bray stood before Justice Day on Friday 2 November 1883 at Durham Assizes, defended by Mr Grainger in what was to be a trial lasting more than ten hours. Although it appeared that there were many people who had known that Bray had done the deed they had all kept silent, some, it was said, through fear of repercussions. There was also the fact that during a miners' strike the people who were detested almost as much as those that had the authority over the mine workers were the scabs or blacklegs who did not give total backing to their work colleagues, so perhaps many thought that Pyle had got what he deserved. Once the police had made extensive enquiries and unravelled the events of that night they summoned many of the witnesses to testify in court. On the day that the murder had taken place Bray had been drinking with his companions at various public houses. Bray and David Liddell had left Durham at about 11 pm to return to Bearpark which was about three miles away. As they walked up Prior's Peth they saw Pyle lying on the grass in a drunken sleep. It was well known that Pyle worked as a blackleg at Ushaw Moor Colliery where there was a strike taking place at that time. As Bray and Liddell walked on they bumped into a group of their acquaintances and one asked if they had seen Pyle as they passed. Bray said they had and they should go back and 'kill the bastard'. When the group of men realised that his threat was serious they urged him to leave Pyle alone but he would not be swayed. Bray broke a rail from the fence before jumping over it and headed towards the defenceless man. It was a dark night and, although the men standing on the path could not see what was taking place, they heard a cry. Realising that Bray had done something to Pyle, the group hurriedly dispersed.

Bray had then gone to his lodgings telling his landlord 'I have put a blackleg through that night.' A few weeks later he had a conversation with an acquaintance in Durham market place, saying, 'when I first struck Pyle he had shouted but I soon put a stop to that'. The two men who had originally helped Pyle on Prior's Peth testified that he had a parcel with him. The parcel was not there when the body was found. Other witnesses stated that Bray was later in possession of a jacket and shirt that did not belong to him and he was also bragging about having money in his pocket. Bray insisted that he was innocent and that the whole affair was a conspiracy with the witnesses committing perjury. He pointed out that there were many of the mining community who would have been hostile towards Pyle because of his actions.

The jury brought in a verdict of guilty and the death sentence was pronounced with Justice Day adding to his summing up that Bray should not look for a reprieve as one would not be granted. It was reported that, after a life of crime, twenty-seven-year-old Peter Bray confessed his sins, admitted his guilt and went to his death penitent. Precautions had been taken to avoid a repeat of the occurrences that had taken place at the previous execution. Once the white hood was in place Bartholomew Binns placed the knot of the noose at the back of the head instead of to the right and the slack of the rope was tied with a thin thread. Bray went to his death on Monday 19 November 1883 with hardly a quiver from the rope.

CHAPTER 30

Murder of a Police Sergeant 1884

On Sunday 24 February 1884 the residents of the small colliery village of Butterknowle were stunned to hear the news that a violent murder had taken place during the previous night near to their homes. Acting Sergeant William Smith of the Durham Constabulary at Barnard Castle had been seen walking his beat at about 9.45 pm and was next seen lying on the road battered and unconscious.

Conflicting records exist as to what actually took place when the body was discovered but, as the discrepancies are minor, one account will be related here. Dr John Jamieson Middleton and his assistant, Dr Gordon Bowker Gorrick, had been for a night out and were on their way home when a young man shouted that a policeman had been murdered. One of the two companions, walking a few steps further, saw Sergeant Smith lying in the road. Middleton ran off after the informant but as he followed was hit in the chest by a stone or brick which was thrown by some men standing on the pit-heap.

The bank leading up to the Diamond Pit at Butterknowle where Sergeant Smith was murdered. The colliery chimney can be seen to the top left of the image.
Author's collection

Fearing for his life, Middleton ran to the bottom of Butterknowle Lane and shouted for help. His cries brought villagers to the scene and in the confusion, although three men thought to be the assailants were seen, it was not known where they had disappeared to. Sergeant Smith was taken to his station but died soon after without regaining consciousness.

On an examination being carried out on the body the injuries sustained were found to be horrific. The skull was severely battered and crushed, teeth were broken and missing and the knees badly bruised and lacerated. The fingers were fractured, probably as the victim had held his hands up in an attempt to defend himself from the onslaught. It was believed that the hapless man had been pelted with stones until he was felled and then, whilst on the ground, attacked with mindless violence. Stones and fragments of bricks were scattered where the attack had taken place and a button was found at the scene which had not come from the deceased's clothing.

The place where the atrocity had been carried out was a narrow track flanked by a steep embankment on one side and a pit-heap on the other. The initial missiles would have been fired from the top of the pit-heap on the unsuspecting victim rendering him defenceless very quickly. It was thought that perhaps the perpetrators intended to

The Diamond Inn at Butterknowle in 2006. It was here the three miners had been drinking on the night of the murder of Sergeant Smith in 1884. The author

throw the body into the disused Diamond Pit before making their getaway but were disturbed before they could do so. It was also believed that the youth that had spoken to Gorrick and Middleton had been one of the perpetrators and, seeing the two men approaching, had alerted them to the victim's plight in order to take the attention from himself and his comrades.

A messenger was sent to alert nearby police who in turn relayed the information to the Barnard Castle police. A sergeant and two constables arrived quickly at the village and, almost immediately, arrested three miners, Joseph Hodgson (aged twenty) Joseph Lowson (twenty-five) and William Siddle (twenty-three). These men had been at a pigeon shoot on the Saturday afternoon and then spent the evening in the Diamond Inn. It was common knowledge that there had been bad blood between the three men and Smith. Siddle had assaulted Smith when he had cause to warn him about his conduct at a gala the previous year, and since then he and his cronies had been heard to utter profanities to the police officer on numerous occasions.

The initial inquests were held at the Royal Oak Inn at Butterknowle, an abundance of witnesses were called as there had been no shortage of people leaving the three nearby inns that night just prior to the victim being found. The clothes of the three men had been taken by

The Royal Oak at Butterknowle in 2006. The initial inquest was held here into the murder of Sergeant Smith in 1884. The author

the police and passed to an analyst for inspection. On Siddle's clothes were marks that were thought to be blood but it could not be proven whether it was from an animal or a human. There was a button missing from Lowson's shirt which matched the one found at the crime scene. Dr Middleton and others had been taken to nearby police stations to look at six or seven men in an identity parade. All pointed out Lowson and Siddle as having the height and build of two of the three men that had been seen near to the scene of the crime. All the evidence was circumstantial and rather flimsy to say the least, nevertheless, it seemed to all fit together rather neatly and, after two days of witness statements, all three men were found guilty and committed for trial.

On Thursday 3 May the three prisoners stood before Justice Hawkins at the Durham Assizes to hear all the witnesses repeat their statements. Mr Skidmore and Mr Walton acted for the prosecution and Mr Lockwood and Mr Greenwell for the defence. Hodgson was found not guilty, Lowson and Siddle guilty. The two men loudly protested their innocence, while at the same time cursing all in authority, but their protests fell on deaf ears as sentence of death was handed down. Hodgson was released and Lowson and Siddle sent back to a cell to await their sentence. There was widespread discontent at the verdict as it was thought by many that all the evidence was purely circumstantial. Siddle wrote a statement in which he pleaded his innocence and laid the blame for the murder squarely on Hodgson and Lowson. Sentence was delayed for a week while a Treasury Official, Mr Cuffe, carried out further investigations on the Home Secretary's instructions. Consequently, Siddle was granted a reprieve. A few days before Lowson was to be executed he made a statement in the prison confessing to the murder. He said that it was not Siddle that had been involved in the attack but Hodgson, and it was he who had struck the first blow. He also stated that Hodgson was a coward not to have come forward and to have let Siddle take the blame.

Sergeant Smith had six children so it would have been meagre comfort to his widow when Joseph Lowson was hanged on Thursday 31 May 1884. James Berry, the executioner, wrote that he had never performed an execution on anyone who showed so much nerve as this terrible man. During the last few days of his life Lowson had exhibited a combination of craven fear and reckless bravado, and his final night was disturbed by periods of terror, shaking as if in a fit. He awoke on his last morning in a seemingly cheerful mood with a bright good morning for the warders and when he stumbled on the walk to the scaffold, laughed hilariously at his own clumsiness. Then, within the final few minutes, his mood darkened and he began to swear using the foulest of language. His voice drowned out the prayers of the chaplain and Lowson died with an oath on his lips.

Siddle was released from custody but was later committed to an insane asylum in which he eventually died. Hodgson was branded a murderer by the locals and would have been shunned by most for the rest of his life.

CHAPTER 31

Malice Aforethought
1888

On Sunday 23 September John Fish was out walking on Birtley Fell when he came across the horribly mutilated body of a woman. A wound inflicted with some kind of long, thin weapon had penetrated her left cheek at an angle, gone through her neck and severed her spinal cord. Her abdomen had been sliced open so deeply that her bowel protruded from the wound. Fish immediately went to the home of Police Constable Dodds, and reported what he had found and then showed the officer where the body was lying. The woman was twenty-two-year-old Jane Beadmore, or Savage, which was the name of her mother's second husband. Dodds had Jane's body moved to her stepfather's house and then sent word to the Gateshead police.

This was the time of the Whitechapel 'Ripper' murders and, because of the nature of the crime, it was widely thought that the same killer had moved north. On a post-mortem being carried out and contact made with those involved in the London slayings it was found there were few similarities. The Whitechapel bodies showed that the killer had anatomical knowledge. The wounds on Jane's body had been inflicted with sheer brute force. Once enquiries began it was quickly established that Jane had been keeping company with a local labourer, William Waddell, who was also twenty-two. On trying to contact him the police discovered that he had left his lodgings at about 7 pm the previous evening and had not returned. On Monday morning Waddell did not appear at the Birtley Iron Works, where he was employed, which was highly unusual. Further enquiries brought information that he and Jane had gone out together at about 8 pm on the Saturday evening.

Waddell's description was sent out to the surrounding areas and word came back that he had been seen in Corbridge on the Sunday so it was assumed that the suspect was travelling north. It was found that at Berwick-on-Tweed Waddell had exchanged his suit for one of poorer quality and 5s (25p) and his billycock hat was swapped for a

A nineteenth century view by Thomas Allom of Berwick. It was here that William Waddell exchanged his suit and cap to disguise himself when he was on the run.
Author's collection

peaked cap. He was eventually recognised at Yetholm, just over the Scottish border, by a farmer, William Stenhouse, and taken into custody. Waddell was transported to Durham gaol to be questioned and for further evidence to be gathered

On 29 November Waddell stood trial at the Durham Winter Assizes before Baron Pollock where he pleaded not guilty. As there had been no witnesses to the actual crime it was up to the prosecution to produce enough circumstantial evidence to prove that Waddell had been the perpetrator. Mrs Savage, Jane's mother, stated that the couple were happy and there were no problems between them. Mrs McCormack, Waddell's landlady, said that he had come into her house after work 'in a state of intoxication' and then left again at about 7 pm. A neighbour, Dorothy Newhall, disputed this saying that Jane had come to her house just after 7 pm with Waddell following her in a few minutes later with 'no sign of a drink in him', although he did seem rather quiet and subdued. The couple left at about 8 pm and Jane was next seen not far from where her body was found. Newark Forster and Henry Brown were moving some furniture on a cart when they saw Jane on the road but saw no one with or near her at the time.

There had still been nothing concrete to show that the man on trial had murdered Jane until Police Constable Thompson took the stand. When Waddell had been recognised at Yetholm, PC Thompson had taken him into custody. On 1 October Waddell had told him that Jane Savage (or Beadmore) was his wife and that when he had left her on Birtley Fell she was dead. Police Constable Sykes of Chester-le-Street then gave evidence to the fact that on 8 October Waddell, who was a large, powerfully-built man, had told him that 'he must have been out of his senses, that he would not strike a woman, much less do a thing like this, when in his senses'. These statements, along with the fact that Waddell had been with Jane on the night she died and that he had run away and tried to disguise himself, were enough to convince the jury of his guilt to premeditated wilful murder and he was sentenced to death. If Waddell had gone to work and carried on as normal he would never have been suspected, much less convicted. There were many people troubled by the verdict as it was felt there was little proof and no confession of guilt. However, on Sunday 16 December Dr Lake, Dean of Durham held an interview with Waddell where he admitted to killing Jane but said it had not been premeditated. He admitted he was drunk at the time and had mutilated the body thinking that would raise suspicion that the murder had been committed by the same person who had carried out the Whitechapel murders. Although now a confessed murderer it was felt by many that Waddell was not in his right mind when he carried out the deed and should not be hanged, but medical examination showed no evidence of insanity.

On the morning of Tuesday 18 December 1888 there was only a small, silent crowd of about fifty people gathered outside the gates of the gaol. As the cathedral clock chimed times the black flag was hoisted showing that James Berry had carried out the sentence of the law on William Waddell. The four members of the press had been placed at some distance where their view of the proceedings was somewhat limited, and then were quickly ushered off the premises without being given the opportunity

The executioner, James Berry, who hanged William Waddell in 1888 for the murder of Jane Beadmore.
Author's collection

to converse with the executioner or any of the prison officials. Immediately after the usual inquest on the body, with the utmost privacy, Berry was taken to the station in a cab by gaol officials and seen onto a train for home.

CHAPTER 32

A Funeral instead of a Wedding
1891

In 1891 John William Johnson had lodged with fifty-two-year-old Margaret Addison at Four Lane Ends, Hetton for eighteen years. Johnson was forty-nine and was employed doing odd jobs on the farms around his local area. Margaret was the widow of William Addison and was known as a decent woman who lived in apparent comfort with her grown up son and daughter. Johnson, on the other hand, was known as a man 'of dissolute habits'. If he had been of a different character perhaps Margaret would have been inclined to accept his romantic advances and this whole sorry affair would have been avoided.

Margaret met and became involved with Andrew Simpson and in early October they announced they were to be married. The thought of losing the woman he loved must have festered in Johnson and over the next few weeks he began to drink even more than he had previously. On Saturday 31 October at about 9 am Johnson had called into the New Inn at Four Lane Ends and had a glass of beer. He had had a conversation with the landlady, Mrs Lamb, who later stated that he was dirty and looked as though he had just come from work. About an hour later he returned to the inn and, after ordering a beer, sat near a window that looked out onto the street.

Margaret had arranged to go and visit her mother in Shincliffe that morning and walked past the window of the inn on her way to the railway station. As she reached the entrance of the station at the end of Springwell Street Johnson left the inn and came up to within a few yards behind her. As he spoke Margaret turned and Johnson produced a gun from behind his back and fired two shots. One shot lodged in his victim's temple and the other in her brow killing her instantaneously. Johnson then walked the few yards to the police station where he calmly told Sergeant Cartwright's wife that he had shot the landlady. Sarah Cartwright asked for the contents of

The railway station at Hetton where Margaret Addison was to catch a train when she was shot by John Johnson in 1891. Author's collection

Johnson's pockets which included a revolver, three cartridges, a knife and some keys. She then put him in a cell, locked the door and sent for her husband.

The trial held in December at Durham Assizes before Justice Wills must have been merely a formality as there were two prosecutors, Mr R Luck and Mr Meek but Johnson admitted guilt and refused any defence. The two witnesses to the event, William Walker, from Easington Lane, and a young girl, Sarah Ellen McCormack had both seen everything that had taken place and gave their statements clearly. Johnson declared that his actions were premeditated so there could be no other verdict that the jury could bring other than guilty of wilful murder which automatically brought sentence of death.

Johnson had no family but was visited on the Friday before his death by a lifelong friend, Thomas Stewart, a miner living at Murton Colliery. It was reported that Johnson had told his friend that he was sorry for what he had done and had made his peace with God and was ready for the consequences. On Tuesday 22 December 1891, having walked calmly and firmly to the scaffold, Johnson, with a prayer on his lips, was hanged by James Billington.

CHAPTER 33

Battered to Death
1898

The last execution to be held at Durham in the nineteenth century was that of thirty-three-year-old Charles Smith for the murder of his twenty-seven-year-old wife, Mary Ann, at Gateshead. Smith was originally from Aberdeen where he had worked for the same firm for ten years. He, his wife, their two children and a five year old nephew had moved to Gateshead early in 1897. The couple had been married nine years with Mary Ann only eighteen when they wed. The family lived at 22 Pipewellgate in an upstairs room which was reached by a small flight of stone steps from the roadway. The next door house was separated by a passageway that led to the river and most of the nearby buildings were warehouses, so these two houses were fairly isolated. The whole area was little more than a slum and the accommodation would have been cramped and unhealthy. Smith was employed as a plasterer and was working on some houses at Jesmond that were being renovated.

On Monday 27 December 1897 Smith and a co-worker left Jesmond at about noon visiting a few public houses on their way home. When they arrived at Smith's home Mary Ann was sitting by the fire partially dressed. She told her husband she had just got out of bed. Smith had brought some beer in with him and they all had a drink before he changed his clothes, picked up his accordion, and left the house. A little the worse for drink Smith returned at about 9 pm when their neighbours, Annie MacDonald and her husband came in and they drank and chatted until about 11 pm. Shortly after midnight Annie heard peculiar noises coming from the Smith's room so, becoming worried, went to investigate. Smith came to the door and said that his 'bonnie wife' was dead. He told her that he had found Mary Ann naked in the water-closet and that someone had murdered her. Annie sent for a doctor and the police.

Within a short time Dr Kay arrived with the police close behind him. It was immediately obvious that Mary Ann was dead and had met her death in violent circumstances. Her body was lying on the bed dressed only in a petticoat with her face so badly battered as to be

Part of the area of Pipewellgate where Charles and Mary Ann Smith lived at the time of the murder in 1898. Author's collection

almost unrecognisable. Her eyes were black and swollen, her lips were bruised and there were numerous cuts that appeared to have bled profusely but the blood had been washed away. In the entire room there was hardly an area that did not have blood spattered over it. It was on the walls, ceiling, pictures and the mirror. The blood on the floor was diluted because there was water mixed with it. The police found a broken broom handle and a block of wood with blood and hair adhered to each. Smith's clothes and face were also blood-smeared. The police went out to the water-closet and found Mary Ann's clothes and blood on the floor. The Smiths had a key to the water-closet as it was only for the use of their family. Smith kept demanding that an investigation be started into who had killed his wife but the police were certain they were looking at the murderer and he was arrested.

Smith was incarcerated in Durham gaol until his trial on Thursday 3 March 1898 before Justice Lawrence. The post-mortem on Mary Ann's body had shown, that besides the injuries to the face, there were numerous cuts and bruises on other parts of the body. The cause of death had been one of two severe head wounds, both of which had exposed the skull.

The Smiths' two boys were questioned and one of them told how his brother and cousin had gone to bed early and he had followed just as the neighbours came in. He had woken later and gone downstairs to find his mother and father in the water-closet. His mother was lying on the floor in just a petticoat. Her eye was bleeding and her back was covered in dirt as if she had been dragged along the floor. The boy said that his mother was mumbling so she must have still been alive at that time. Smith then took hold of Mary Ann's head and the son took her legs and they carried her upstairs and put her on the floor. Smith washed her chest using a dish of water then lifted her onto the bed. The boy said that his mother had pawned some of his father's clothes earlier in the week and Smith had been very angry. When Smith had come in at about 9 pm on the night Mary Ann died they had started arguing again and she had thrown a bottle at him which had glanced of his head leaving a small cut which was how there came to be blood on the mirror. This had happened just before the MacDonalds had come in for a drink.

Smith had no defence against his actions because he insisted he had been so drunk he could remember nothing of that night. He stated he loved his wife and would never have knowingly hurt her. Because

An outside water-closet such as the one at the rear of the Smith's home in Pipewellgate. Author's collection

of the child's statement the jury had no choice but to find Smith guilty of murder but they added a strong recommendation for mercy because of the circumstances. Justice Lawrence donned the black cap and passed sentence of death.

A petition requesting a reprieve was drawn up and signed by many notable people in Aberdeen who had known Smith for many years as a man of good character. This was sent to the Home Secretary along with the recommendation for mercy by the jury.

The day prior to the date set for his execution Smith was told that the Home Secretary had refused to interfere so there was to be no reprieve. His day must have brightened a little when he was allowed to see his eleven-year-old son. It was reported that it gave Smith peace of mind to be told that this boy was to be taken in and looked after by the Dr Barnardo's Home for Waifs and Strays (what became of his other son and his nephew remains unclear). Other arrivals at the gaol that day were the executioner James Billington with his son, Thomas, as assistant. They immediately inspected the rope and the new and permanent scaffold that had been erected within the gaol.

On Tuesday 22 March 1898, led by the chaplain reading the service for the dead, the small entourage made their way to the scaffold. Three members of the press had been granted permission to watch the proceedings. Their later reports stated that Smith walked with a firm step and from reaching the scaffold to the moment of death was only a minute in total.

Chronology of Executions

1711 Thursday 13 August: Thomas Wilson, John Brady, Andrew Miller, Andrew Langland and Robert Evans for breaking into the house of William Storey, a miller at Hedley on Friday 19 December 1710. They stole 10 guineas in gold, £59.5s in money and valuables.

1725 Monday 20 August: Thomas Charlton of Birtley, North Tyne in Northumberland had induced Elizabeth Whatoff to marry him although he already had a wife living in London. He had fired a pistol and committed other acts of violence towards Elizabeth leaving her for dead and stealing her money and other valuables. Charlton's only plea to defence was he could not get rid of Elizabeth and was forced to marry her.

An etching depicting Durham in the eighteenth century. Author's collection

1726 Saturday 3 August: Stephen Browne, Arthur Hewetson, David Steele, Ann Bone and Jane Browne for robbing John Marshall of thirty-two guineas on the King's Highway in the parish of Jarrow on Thursday 3 June.

1727 July: William Stephenson, a grocer of Northallerton, for throwing Mary Farding, who was pregnant by him, into the sea near the rock formation known locally as Maiden's Bower at Hartlepool. This rock stood just north of the East Battery. The churchwarden's accounts dated 7 June 1727 read 'for making Mary Farding's grave 1s 10d unpaid'.

1732 Saturday 23 August: John and James Graham for horse stealing. James Graham was baptized on the morning of his execution at the church of St Mary-le-Bow, a part of the old gaol being within that parish.

1739 Saturday 5 September: Thomas Galilee for horse stealing.

1748 Thursday 15 August: Paul Coleman for robbing Mr Hutchinson, an attorney, of his watch and horse and for stopping Mr Colling on Elvet Moor with the intent to rob. Mr Hutchinson's horse was found near Plawsworth and when Coleman's lodgings were searched pistols, powders and flints were found. It was determined that Coleman had come from London to the North with the specific purpose of highway robbery and house-breaking.

Maiden's Bower at Hartlepool where William Stephenson threw his pregnant mistress, Mary Farding, into the sea in 1727. Author's collection

The twelfth century church of St Hilda in Hartlepool where Mary Farding was interred. The author

1750   Thursday 27 August: James Macfidum, alias Macfarlane, for robbing Robert Hopes, a boy of about ten. Hopes had been walking across Whickham Common on his way to school when a man and woman, who were later found to be part of a Faw gang (men and women who roamed the area stealing whatever they could) had stopped him. Macfidum half stripped the boy and threatened to cut his throat if he shouted for help.

1757   Monday 8 August: William Heugh for the murder of a bastard child.

1762   Monday 9 August: Thomas Coulson for the murder of Thomas Byers.

1763   Monday 1 August: Margaret Middleton, alias Coulson, had been employed to take a pauper child, Lucy Elliott, alias Curry, to a new home in Northallerton. Middleton was paid in advance but she drowned the child in the River Browney near Sunderland Bridge on Friday 24 June.

1768   John Steads for robbery.

1773   Monday 23 August: John Coltman, Richard Preston, Francis Dixon and Matthew Vasey were tried at Durham Assizes before Sir William Blackstone and Sir Henry Gould. They were charged with robbing a Jew in Darlington of ninety guineas. Vasey was found guilty and hanged at Durham.

A view of Browney Lane Bridge, Sunderland. It was in this river that Margaret Middleton drowned the infant Lucy Elliot in 1763. The author

The town of Barnard Castle where John Moses stole a quantity of drapery goods in 1803. Author's collection

1776 Thursday 15 August: Joseph Humphries, aged about twenty-six, for housebreaking at Sunderland and stealing £14.4s.6d. He went to his death protesting his innocence of the crime.

1781 Monday 20 August: John Tully for robbing and violently beating Mr Mills of Moormills.

Tuesday 20 November: Margaret Tinkler for recommending certain means to kill an infant. Both baby and mother, Jane Parkinson, died. Tinkler told a clergyman and a surgeon that she had only recommended the means and it was Parkinson who had carried out the act. When Tinkler's body was dissected at Whitesmocks, near Durham, two long, wire hair pins were found in her stomach and it was assumed that she had swallowed them to take her own life.

1783 Monday 18 August: Robert Storey for murder. Thomas Idle, known as Cockle Geordie, had been a cockle-seller and had unwisely shown a roll of guineas in a public house. Storey had lain in wait, robbed and murdered him.

1785 Monday 25 July: John Winship for the murder of his maid-servant by administering drugs to procure an abortion.

Monday 1 August: William Hamilton and his wife, Isabella, for robbing the house of John Smith of Stobbalee near Witton Gilbert and for cruelly using Smith and his wife.

On the same day Thomas Elliott was hanged for horse-stealing and Duncan Wright for housebreaking.

1786 Monday 21 August: Francis Blenkinsopp and Morley Tewitt for house-breaking.

Thursday 30 August: Henry Jennings for horse-stealing.

1802 Monday 23 August: John Carleton for firing a loaded pistol at Thomas Greenwell, a grocer, when he and his accomplices tried to enter the grocer's premises in Gateshead forcibly. Carleton's defence said there was no ball in the pistol so murder was not intended however, a week after the execution, the ball was found imbedded in a wall of the shop.

1803 Monday 15 August: John Moses for stealing a quantity of drapery goods from the shop of Benjamin Jackson in Barnard Castle.

1805 Monday 2 August: Richard Metcalfe for the murder of his son-in-law.

1816 Saturday 17 August: John Grieg, aged thirty-seven, for the murder of Elizabeth Stonehouse of Monkwearmouth. He had the dubious honour of being the first person to be executed in front of the new county courthouse.

An early view of Raby Castle, situated near Bishop Auckland, the home of the Duke of Cleveland, when his whipper-in was murdered in 1848. Author's collection

1819 Monday 12 April: George Atcheson, aged sixty-seven, for raping Isabella Ramshaw. The child was under ten years of age. It was recorded that he was very penitent and hoped his death might deter others from such a crime.

1822 Monday 18 March: Henry Anderson, pitman of Old Painsher, for a rape on Sarah Armstrong.

1848 Saturday 25 March: William Thompson for the murder near Barnard Castle of John Shirley, head whipper-in to the Duke of Cleveland, on 2 February.

Sources

John Sykes, *Local Records of Remarkable Events which have occurred in Northumberland and Durham, Newcastle Upon Tyne and Berwick on Tweed,* Volumes I–II, 1833.

T Fordyce, *Local Records of Remarkable Events which have occurred in Northumberland and Durham, Newcastle Upon Tyne and Berwick on Tweed,* Volumes III–IV, 1867–76.

W H D Longstaffe, *The History & Antiquities of Darlington,* 1854.

James Berry, *My Experiences as an Executioner,* 1892.

Geoffrey Abbott, *William Calcraft Executioner Extra-Ordinaire,* 2002.

Newspapers
Durham Advertiser
Durham Chronicle
South Durham and Cleveland Mercury
South Durham Herald
Stockton and Hartlepool Mercury
Northern Daily Mail
Newcastle Weekly Chronicle

168

Index

Places
Aberdeen 160
Albert Hill 77, 79, 98
Allan Arms 81
All Saint's Church 59
Alnwick 32
Annfield Plain 101–2

Baddow 10
Baine's Lane 130
Barnard Castle 98, 116–9, 148, 164–6
Bearpark 144
Benwell's Public House
Berwick-on-Tweed 151–2
Birtley 161
Birtley Fell 151
Birtley Iron Works 151
Bishop Auckland 85, 129, 166
Bishopwearmouth 30
Black Fell 44
Black Horse 121
Blaydon 55–6
Bradford 12
Brancepeth 59–60
Brandon 142
Brecondykes 62–3
Bridgegate 116–7
Broadmires 66
Boldon Colliery 44
Butcher's Arms 130
Butterknowle 129, 146–8

Carrick's Beer House 84
Castle Garth 143
Chelmsford 10
Chester-le-Street 44, 59, 69, 97
Church Street 113, 115
Cleveland Street 98–100
Cockfield 128
Consett 104, 108
Coronation Street 130
Crossgate Peth 142

Darlington 26, 35–6, 77, 79, 81, 98, 113–4, 163
Dent's Hole 31–2
Diamond Inn 147–8
Diamond Pit 146, 148
Dipton Colliery 108
Dobson's Beer House 118
Dodd's Beer House 102
Drewitt's Buildings 51
Dryburn 14
Dudley 11
Duncombe Street 83
Dun Cow Inn 137–9

East Rainton Colliery 87
Edmondsley 121
Elsdon 45
Elvet 14
Evenwood 128–31